Twayne's United States Authors Series

EDITOR OF THIS VOLUME

Kenneth Eble
University of Utah

Thornton Wilder
(Second Edition)

TUSAS 5

Thornton Wilder

THORNTON WILDER

Second Edition

By REX BURBANK

San Jose State University

TWAYNE PUBLISHERS
A DIVISION OF G. K. HALL & CO., BOSTON

Library of Congress Cataloging in Publication Data

Burbank, Rex J.
  Thornton Wilder.

  (Twayne's United States Authors Series; TUSAS 5)
  Bibliography: p. 141 - 45
  Includes index.
  1. Wilder, Thornton Niven, 1897 - 1975—Criticism and inter-
pretation.
PS3545.I345Z57   1978   813'.5'2   77-26237
ISBN 0-8057-7223-5

Contents

About the Author

Preface

Acknowledgments

Chronology

1. Backgrounds   17
2. Three Romance Novels   30
3. Toward an American Perspective   55
4. Three Theatricalist Plays   70
5. Existentialism and Humanism   97
6. Final Entries   115
7. Limitations and Achievement   127
   Notes and References   137
   Selected Bibliography   141
   Index   146

About the Author

Rex Burbank is Professor of English at San Jose State University (California), where he has taught since 1959 and served at various times as Associate Graduate Dean and Dean of the Faculty. He earned both undergraduate and graduate degrees at the University of Michigan, taking his doctorate under the guidance of the late Joe Lee Davis. In 1968 - 69 he lectured as Fulbright Professor at Thammasat and Chulalongkorn Universities in Bangkok, Thailand. His publications include *Sherwood Anderson* (Twayne) and (with Jack B. Moore) a three-volume anthology of American literature (Merrill).

Preface

Critical and popular recognition came suddenly to Thornton Wilder with the publication in 1927 of *The Bridge of San Luis Rey*. A bestseller almost immediately after it first appeared, *The Bridge* went through thirteen printings in England, had sales of over 250 thousand copies in its first year alone, and won the Pulitzer Prize for its author in 1928.

Success of *The Bridge* with both the public and the critics is not hard to account for, since it represented a radical and welcome departure from the realism that dominated the fiction of the 1920s. Critic Harry Salpeter wrote in *Outlook* in 1928 that readers of fiction "were tired of realistic novels and were rotten ripe for a book like *The Bridge*, whether they knew it or not,"[1] and St. John Adcock declared that the book represented a healthy change from the "naive school" of realism that dwelt inordinately upon the grosser aspects of life. *The Bridge*, Adcock added with approval, portrayed "those equally real human qualities that help distinguish man from four-legged animals" and restored that "sense of mystery of life" lacking in the realistic fiction of the day.[2] Critics admired its stylistic clarity and gentleness of tone as well as its nonrealistic matter. Arnold Bennett said in the London *Evening Standard* that he was "dazzled" by Wilder's performance and added: "The writing, simple, straight, just and powerful, has not been surpassed in the recent epoch."[3] And Alexander Woollcott, whose lifelong admiration for Wilder began with *The Bridge*, described it as a "novel of aloof and untruckling beauty."[4]

The Bridge immediately put Wilder in the front rank of writers, and he enjoyed two years of widespread critical approval; even his first novel—*The Cabala*, published in 1926—received renewed attention and respect. But with the publication in 1930 of his third novel, *The Woman of Andros*, a critical reaction occurred: it was an unpropitious time for the appearance of a novel that took place in pre-Christian Greece and involved the melancholy longings of an Andrian hetaera for religious certitude. Wall Street had collapsed with the stock market crash in 1929, and lines of the unemployed were becoming appallingly long. As it became apparent that a full-scale depression was under way, the conviction grew among both critics and general readers that it was the responsibility of the writer to portray realistically and uncompromisingly the social problems of his country and his time.

While not everyone agreed with the Marxists that novelists should depict the class conflict—the struggle between the workers and the bosses—demand for a literature that was grounded in social realism was increasing. Remoteness of *The Woman of Andros* from the social problems of America, 1930, left Wilder vulnerable, therefore, to charges that he was either indifferent to them or unable to confront them. *The Cabala*, which took place in Rome, and *The Bridge*, whose action was set in seventeenth-century Peru, were only slightly less remote than *The Woman;* and the three-minute plays in *The Angel That Troubled the Waters* (1928), based in large part upon Classical Greek and biblical myths, were even further removed. Works that only two years before had been timely departures from a too-realistic literary milieu were now considered superciliously indifferent to the real facts of life.

The first and most serious critical attack against Wilder in this period came on October 22, 1930, when the *New Republic* published an article by Michael Gold titled "Wilder: Prophet of the Genteel Christ." Gold accused Wilder of scornfully ignoring the social injustices in America and of writing for a "small sophisticated class." "Is Mr. Wilder a Swede or a Greek, or is he an American?" he demanded. "No stranger would know from the books he has written." He complained that Wilder "has all the virtues Veblen said this leisure class would demand: glossy high finish as against intrinsic qualities, conspicuous inutility, caste feeling, love of the archaic, etc. . . . This Emily Post of culture will never reproach them; or remind them of Pittsburgh or the breadlines." He charged that Wilder's religion "isn't the fervent religion of the Holy Rollers or Baptists or Tolstoy or Dostoyevsky. It is Anglo-Catholicism, that last refuge of the American snob . . . it is that newly fashionable literary religion that centers around Jesus Christ, the First British Gentleman."

Gold's attack set off a controversy that brought hundreds of letters to the *New Republic*, "some carefully reasoned, some violent, and almost hysterical," as Malcolm Cowley wrote later in *Exile's Return*. Generally, the weight of responsible criticism was on Wilder's side, for Henry Hazlitt defended him in *The Nation*,[5] Edmund Wilson in the *New Republic*.[6] And when the quarrel ended, it was evident—Cowley wrote in retrospect—that Gold had "ridiculously overstated his case; he had failed to see that Wilder was a serious writer preoccupied with moral problems and that they were our own problems, even though Wilder's characters were disguised in Peruvian or Greek Costumes. . . ."[7]

But while Wilder retained a large popular following and the approval of a good many able critics, the Gold dispute had the unhappy effect of making the critics cautious about showing enthusiasm for him. Many of them had been too profuse in their admiration of his "aesthetic" qualities; and, with the onset of the depression, they were not prepared to make a case for fiction that said nothing about slum conditions, unemployment, or absentee ownership. As a result, Wilder got little attention for the next eight years.

But then, with the success of *Our Town* in 1938 and *The Skin of Our Teeth* in 1942—for each won Wilder a Pulitzer Prize—the critical pattern of lavish praise followed by attack and, finally, neglect or indifference was repeated. Like *The Bridge*, *Our Town* and *The Skin of Our Teeth* were timely. *Our Town* was staged at a time when Americans were beginning to rediscover their democratic heritage after their disillusionment with the shabby materialism and the subsequent economic paralysis the nation had fallen into in the twenties and thirties. *The Skin of Our Teeth* appeared just after the outbreak of World War II, when disaster seemed imminent. Both plays were affirmative in spirit and were well received at least partly because they answered the need of the times for affirmation.

However, in 1942 another controversy, nearly as violent as the Gold dispute twelve years before, developed when Joseph Campbell and Henry Morton Robinson, then making their "key" to James Joyce's *Finnegans Wake*, discovered that Wilder had borrowed much of his material for *Skin* from the Joyce novel. In a series of articles appearing in the *Saturday Review* under the title "The Skin of Whose Teeth?" Campbell and Robinson drew parallels between the two works in characters, structure, and style; and, in effect, they accused Wilder of plagiarism. Like Gold, they ridiculously overstated their case. They confused Wilder's indebtedness to Joyce with deceitful appropriation of Joyce's material; but the effect of their attack was the same as that of Gold's. When the controversy was over, critics, seemingly exhausted by the subject of Wilder, gave him scant attention for the next decade.

This peculiar critical history resulted in a failure, or reluctance, by critics to explore Wilder's art, and certain stock attitudes persisted—and still persist. It is still fashionable in some quarters to regard him as a schoolbook author whose works have the kind of perspicuity, didacticism, and tearful optimism that makes them suitable for high-school anthologies but not material for critical analysis. Among a good many critics who ought to know better a belief remains that because he has had popular success Wilder has sinned against their critical rule of thumb that an author cannot be good if he is popular. The assumptions behind these views have enough truth in them to be troublesome. Wilder's works—particularly *The Bridge, Our Town, The Matchmaker,* and "The Happy Journey"—have the ingredients that appeal to young audiences and are widely read or enacted in the schools. Moreover, he does take a more optimistic attitude toward life than most of his contemporary writers. And he has been popular.

But even if we concede the charges against him, there still remains plenty in Wilder's works to engage the mind of the sophisticated reader who expects more than amusement from literary art. Controversy over his novels and plays seems likely to continue in the future as it did almost until the day, December 7, 1975, Wilder died. Richard Goldstone's largely sympathetic but not uncritical *Thornton Wilder: An Intimate Portrait,* published shortly before Wilder's death, prompted a heated rejoinder in a *New York Times* review by Malcolm Cowley, who accused Goldstone of making essentially the same charges against Wilder that Gold had made thirty-five years before.[8] Both Goldstone and Cowley agreed, however, that Wilder's fiction and dramas warrant serious critical study—an assumption that is the basis of this book.

REX BURBANK

San Jose State University

Acknowledgments

I am deeply grateful for the help I had while writing this book. Isabel Wilder, sister of Thornton Wilder, was kind and generous in providing me with valuable information about her brother and his work. Wilder himself made available materials—including the unpublished *The Alcestiad*—I could not otherwise have obtained. I am particularly indebted to the late Professor Joe Lee Davis of the University of Michigan for his discerning criticism of my work, his suggestions, and his encouragement. Kenneth Rowe, Carlton Wells, and Fred Walcott gave generously of their interest, perceptive comments, and advice. I have been fortunate in the help I have received, but I am of course responsible myself for any errors in fact or faults in judgment.

I wish to make special acknowledgment for permission to quote from the following works still in copyright:

To Harper and Brothers for permission to quote from *Heaven's My Destination, Our Town, The Skin of Our Teeth, The Matchmaker,* and *The Ides of March* by Thornton Wilder; and from *Spiritual Problems in Contemporary Literature,* edited by Stanley Romaine Hopper.

To the *American Scholar* for permission to quote from "Thornton Wilder: 'The Notation of the Heart' " by Edmund Fuller, which appeared in the spring, 1959, issue.

To Harcourt, Brace and Company for the passage from *Selected Essays 1917 - 1932* by T. S. Eliot, copyright, 1932, by Harcourt, Brace and Company, Inc.; renewed, 1960, by T. S. Eliot. Reprinted by permission of the publishers.

To Holt, Rinehart and Winston, Inc. for permission to quote from John Gassner's *Form and Idea in Modern Theatre* and from Paul Cubeta's *Modern Drama for Analysis.*

To The Viking Press, Inc. for permission to quote from Malcolm Cowley's *Exile's Return.*

To Princeton University Press for permission to quote from Wilder's "Thoughts on Playwrighting," in *The Intent of the Artist,* edited by Augusto Centeno; and from Paul Elmer More's *On Being Human.*

To Albert and Charles Boni, Inc., Publishers, for permission to quote from *The Cabala, The Bridge of San Luis Rey,* and *The Woman of Andros* by Thornton Wilder.

To Coward-McCann, Inc. for permission to quote from *The Angel That Troubled the Waters, The Long Christmas Dinner and Other Plays* by Thornton Wilder.

To *The Saturday Review* for permission to quote from Ross Parmenter's "Novelist into Playwright," which appeared in the June, 1938, issue.

To Random House for permission to quote from Wilder's Introduction to *The Geographical History of America* by Gertrude Stein.

And to Thornton Wilder for permission to quote from "James Joyce (1882 - 1941)," which appeared in the March, 1941, issue of *Poetry: A Magazine of Verse,* and from *The Alcestiad.*

Chronology

1897   April 17, born in Madison, Wisconsin.

1906   Lives six months in Hong Kong during father's term (1906 - 1909) as American Consul General. Attends a German school.

1906 -   Resides and attends public schools in Berkeley, California;
1911   lives in Shanghai, where father has been transferred. Attends a German school briefly in Shanghai, then is a student for a year and a half at the China Inland Mission School at Chefoo.

1912 -   Attends Thacher School, Ojai, California.
1913

1913 -   Attends and graduates from Berkeley High School.
1915

1915 -   Enters Oberlin College, Ohio. Early works, including some
1917   plays later in *The Angel That Troubled the Waters*, appear in the *Oberlin Literary Magazine*.

1917 -   Transfers to Yale. Family living near New Haven.
1918   Publishes short plays and essays in the *Yale Literary Magazine*.

1918 -   Summer work for War Industries Board, Washington, D.C.
1919   Turned down by various services because of his eyes, but finally accepted by Coast Artillery. Serves as corporal in First Coast Artillery, Fort Adams, Rhode Island, for eight months.

1919 -   Returns to Yale. On editorial board of *Yale Literary*
1920   *Magazine*. First long play, *The Trumpet Shall Sound*, published serially in *YLM*. Receives B.A. from Yale.

1920 -   Studies archaeology—though not enrolled in courses—at
1921   the American Academy in Rome. Begins writing *The Cabala*.

1920 -   Teaches French at the Lawrenceville School, New Jersey.
1924   1924, publishes *Three Sentences* (from *The Cabala*) in *The Double Dealer* (New Orleans, Louisiana); and *A Diary: First and Last Entry* in *S4N* (New Haven)—first

publications in nonacademic periodicals. Spring 1924, takes leave of absence to attend Princeton Graduate School.

1925   First of several summers spent writing at MacDowell Colony, Peterborough, New Hampshire. Receives M.A. in French literature. Begins writing *The Bridge of San Luis Rey*. Goes to Europe to work on *The Bridge*.

1926   *The Trumpet Shall Sound* directed and produced in New York at the Laboratory Theatre by Richard Boleslavsky. *The Cabala* published, fall.

1927 - Returns to Lawrenceville as Housemaster of the Davis
1928   House, 1927. *The Bridge of San Luis Rey* published, November 1927. Receives Pulitzer Prize for *The Bridge*, 1928. *The Angel That Troubled the Waters* published, 1928. Resigns from Lawrenceville, June 1928; goes to Europe to finish *The Woman of Andros*.

1929 - Makes a cross-country lecture tour. *The Woman of Andros*
1930   published, 1930.

1930 - Lectures in comparative literature at University of
1936   Chicago, half of each year. Makes lecture tours and works for several five- to six-week periods at various motion-picture studios in Hollywood.

1931   *The Long Christmas Dinner and Other Plays*. Translates and adapts André Obey's *Le Viol de Lucrèce* for actress Katharine Cornell. Produced in New York by Guthrie McClintic, music by Deems Taylor.

1933   *Lucrèce* published.

1935   Meets Gertrude Stein, who is lecturing at the University of Chicago. Spends one term as visiting professor at the University of Hawaii. *Heaven's My Destination* published.

1937   Translates and adapts Ibsen's *A Doll's House* for actress Ruth Gordon. Produced and directed by Jed Harris.

1938   *Our Town* given first performance in Princeton, New Jersey, January 22. Plays a week in Boston. Opens February 4 in New York. Awarded Pulitzer Prize. *The Merchant of Yonkers* first produced, Boston, December 12; opens in New York, directed by Max Reinhardt, starring Jane Cowl, December 28.

1938   *The Merchant of Yonkers*.

1941   Essay on James Joyce published in *Poetry: A Magazine of Verse*.

1942   Writes script for Alfred Hitchcock film, *The Shadow of a*

Doubt. Enlists in U.S. Air Force, commissioned a captain after training in Air Intelligence School. *The Skin of Our Teeth* produced by Michael Myerberg at Shubert Theatre, New York, November; directed by Elia Kazan with Tallulah Bankhead, Frederic March, and Florence Eldridge.

1942 -
1943
Serves in African Theatre of War. Receives a third Pulitzer Prize, for *The Skin of Our Teeth*, 1943. Stationed in Caeserta, Italy; promoted to lieutenant-colonel.

1944 -
1945
Returns to U.S. Revival of *Our Town* at City Center, New York, 1944. Separated from military service, September, 1945.

1946
American production of *Our Town*, directed by Jed Harris, opens in London at the New Theatre, April.

1948
The Ides of March.

1949
Lectures at the Goethe Festival in Aspen, Colorado.

1950 -
1951
Holds Charles Eliot Norton Professorship of Poetry at Harvard, lecturing on Thoreau, Poe, Melville, Emily Dickinson, Whitman in series titled "The American Characteristics in Classic American Literature."

1952
Awarded Gold Medal for Fiction by the American Academy of Arts and Letters.

1954 -
1956
The Matchmaker (revised text of *The Merchant of Yonkers*) performed at Edinburgh Festival, Scotland, August 1954, directed by Tyrone Guthrie, with Ruth Gordon as Dolly Levi. Plays a year in London and a year in New York. 1955, *The Alcestiad* (called *A Life in the Sun* during its opening run) performed at the Edinburgh Festival in August. *The Skin of Our Teeth*, starring Helen Hayes and Mary Martin, sent to Paris by U.S. State Department for the *Salut à la France* festivities.

1959
Opening of French language production of *The Matchmaker*, National Theatre, Brussels, Belgium. Opening of German language production of *Die Alkestiade*, Schausspielhaus, Zurich, Switzerland.

1961
Opera libretto *The Long Christmas Dinner*, music by Paul Hindemith, presented at Mannheim, Germany.

1962
Opening at the Circle-in-the-Square Theatre, Bleecker Street, New York, of three one-act plays, January 11: "Someone from Assisi," from the cycle *The Seven Deadly Sins;* "Infancy" and "Childhood," from *The Seven Ages of*

Man; all given the general title for this production, directed by José Quintero, *Plays for Bleecker Street.* World premiere of *The Alcestiad* (operatic version), libretto by Wilder, music by Louise Talma, in German as *Die Alkestiade,* Frankfurt, Germany, March. April 30, "An Evening with Thornton Wilder," Washington, D.C. —Wilder reading from his works as guest of President Kennedy's cabinet. May 20, retires to Arizona to write.

1963   Awarded U.S. Presidential Medal of Freedom.

1964   *Hello, Dolly!,* musical comedy version of *The Matchmaker,* produced on stage.

1965   Awarded National Medal of Literature.

1967   *The Eighth Day.*

1968   Wins National Book Award for *The Eighth Day.*

1973   *Theophilus North.*

1975   Dies December 7.

1977   *The Alcestiad* published posthumously.

CHAPTER 1

Backgrounds

IN an interview with a *Time* reporter in 1953, Wilder observed wryly that he was the only American writer of his generation "who did not 'go to Paris' " during the 1920s.[1] Though true only in a figurative sense, his comment emphasized the differences between himself and most of his contemporaries. Unlike those who "went to Paris" in this figurative sense, he did not become a voluntary exile from America. He shared their admiration for Europe, its cultural treasures, its freer, more hospitable and stimulating atmosphere, and he deplored, as they did, the trivializing absorption with gadgetry, the business mentality, and the puritanical moralism that kept the United States in a state of cultural arrest; but he did not make the symbolic break with his homeland that so many other writers and artists made in the 1920s. In fact, he was a rarity among the better writers of his time in not being "alienated"; while he felt uncomfortable with certain aspects of modern industrial civilization, he maintained a hopeful attitude toward the possibilities of democratic culture, and when he himself "went to Paris" (as he often did), he went as a visitor but never as a *déraciné*, or exile.[2]

But Wilder's comment to the *Time* reporter acknowledged not only personal differences between himself and his more rebellious contemporaries; more importantly, it stressed the fundamental, long-standing distinctions between his written works and those of writers in the mainstreams of American writing as represented by F. Scott Fitzgerald, Ernest Hemingway, John Dos Passos, and William Faulkner among novelists, and Eugene O'Neill, Robert Sherwood, and Elmer Rice among dramatists. He understood the risks involved in taking the route less traveled by, but he chose his course early, and stayed on it despite enormous critical pressures to change. Going his own way saved him from being identified with the "schools" of realism, naturalism, symbolism, and a number of others; but that

17

freedom cost him the critical attention that accompanies recognizable affinities with other writers who are currently in favor, or with literary movements. His novels and plays comprised a curious combination of the traditional and innovative, provincial and urbane, modern and Classical, American and European, timely and timeless—by careful design. Those qualities made him one of the most popular authors of the twentieth century but deprived him of the approbation—especially among academic critics—enjoyed by Hemingway, O'Neill, and others of his generation of serious writers. A humanist with a strong religious bent, a dramatist and novelist who used traditional literary forms in new ways, Wilder presented difficult but fascinating problems almost from the beginning of his career not only for those who did not care for his work but for those who found it rewarding and worthy of rigorous critical scrutiny. As his remark to the *Time* reporter implies, he was aware of his uniqueness and the risks it entailed, but he refused to change his course. A brief look at his early life will help explain why he became at once the most traditional and the most innovative—and certainly the most controversial—American writer of his time.

I   The Early Years: Madison to New Haven

Thornton Niven Wilder was born on April 17, 1897, in Madison, Wisconsin, where his father, Amos P. Wilder, was editor of the *Wisconsin State Journal.* Amos P. Wilder was a devout Congregationalist who inherited his Puritan conscience and dedication to duty from his New England Calvinist ancestors. His wife, Isabella, was the daughter of the Reverend Doctor Thornton M. Niven, pastor of the Presbyterian Church of Dobbs Ferry, New York. Their first child, Amos N. Wilder, was born in 1895; he was to become a distinguished professor of theology at Harvard University and write on the spiritual aspects of contemporary literature. Three daughters, Charlotte, Isabel, and Janet, were born in 1898, 1900 and 1910, respectively; Isabel would later give up her own promising career as a writer to become Thornton's confidant and frequent traveling companion, and to take charge of his voluminous correspondence. Another son, Thornton's twin, died at birth.

Upon graduation from Yale in 1884, Amos P. Wilder worked as a journalist in New Haven while he studied for his doctorate in political science. He continued with newspaper work for two years in New York after taking his degree in 1892, then married and moved to Madison. A supporter of Theodore Roosevelt, he was appointed consul general to Hong Kong in 1906, and in 1909 was transferred to Shanghai. Isabella and the children accompanied him to Hong Kong but stayed only six months before returning to the United States and settling in Berkeley, California, where she lived alone with the children while they attended the public schools. In 1910, the family rejoined him in Shanghai, and Thornton was sent for a short time to a German school in Shanghai and then to the China Inland Mission School at Chefoo. It soon became clear that Thornton would be better educated and happier at a different school, and in 1912 he was enrolled with his brother Amos at the Thacher School in Ojai, California.

According to Wilder's biographer, Richard Goldstone, Thornton was shy, withdrawn, and bookish during his early boyhood years at school, but friends at the Thacher School remembered him as lively and extroverted. His scholastic record at Ojai was no better than average. He had little taste for the horseback riding he was required to endure, and he shared none of his brother's athletic ability. Yet he seemed to enjoy the friendships acquired there, many of which lasted for life. In 1913 he returned to Berkeley, where his performance in school improved substantially during the first year but declined again when he became captivated by the stage plays at the Liberty Theatre in Oakland. At about this time he began writing dramas of his own.

Thornton hoped to attend Yale after graduating from Berkeley High School in 1915, but his father sent him to Oberlin College in Ohio instead. Despite his initial disappointment, he found Oberlin a stimulating place where his interests in theatre, music, and classical literature were encouraged and where for the first time he found adults besides his mother who appreciated his growing creative talents and intellectual curiosity. He studied the Greek masterpieces and Virgil and Dante, in translation, in a course offered by "the greatest lecturer I have ever heard," Professor Charles H. A. Wager. He was invited to read his plays and stories in Wager's home; and he enjoyed a lively responsiveness to his religious ideas in the home of Professor William Hutchins, whose son Robert Maynard Hutchins became Wilder's lifelong friend. The warm, humane atmosphere of Oberlin also nourished the growing gregariousness that was to become a notable part of his personality; and in that invigorating environment he began to publish some of his writings in the *Oberlin Literary Magazine*.

By the end of the school year in 1917 the Wilder family had moved to New Haven, Connecticut, where Amos P. Wilder was connected with Yale University, and Thornton enrolled at Yale that fall. He published a number of short plays and essays in the *Yale Literary Magazine* during his first year but dropped out of school to serve in the Coast Artillery for eight months in 1918 - 19 at Fort Adams, Rhode Island, before completing his senior year in 1920. That final undergraduate year saw the publication, serially, of his first full-length play, *The Trumpet Shall Sound*, in the *Yale Literary Magazine*.

After graduation, Wilder spent several months in Rome, taking, without actually enrolling in, courses in archaeology at the American Academy. Toward the end of his stay there, he began to write his first novel, a tale about a group of Roman aristocrats whose lives suggest the decline of the old order in Europe. He gave his draft the working title *Memoirs of a Roman Student;* when completed, the novel was to be titled *The Cabala*. Though *The Cabala* was not published in its entirety until 1926, a section of it, called "Three Sentences," appeared in the New Orleans *Double Dealer* in September 1924. Along with a short story, "A Diary: First and Last Entry," which came out in a New Haven periodical, *S4N*, in February 1924, it represented the only short fiction he was ever to publish in nonacademic publications.

While Thornton was in Rome his father found a position for him as a teacher of French at the Lawrenceville School in Princeton, New Jersey, a job he held for four years before resigning to work on a master's degree in French at Princeton and—more importantly to him—too complete *The Cabala* and get started on other works. Encouraged by publisher Albert Boni, Wilder finished *The Cabala* in December 1925. With its publication by Albert and Charles Boni the following fall, Wilder's career as a novelist was under way. That same fall, on the recommendation of *Theatre Arts Monthly* editor Edith Isaacs, Richard Boleslavsky, director of the American Laboratory Theatre, produced *The Trumpet Shall Sound*. Though the effort failed and Wilder was later to discourage even the reading of the play, Boleslavsky's production was the first important staging of Wilder's work, and it launched his career as a dramatist.

Wilder began to write *The Bridge of San Luis Rey* shortly after he completed *The Cabala* and while he was doing graduate work at Princeton in late 1925. He received his M.A. the following June and went to Europe in the fall, where he met and became friends with

Ernest Hemingway, who, like Wilder, had not as yet "arrived."[3] He made notes for *The Bridge* while in Europe, then returned to the United States in the spring of 1927 and finished it that summer at the MacDowell Colony. With its publication in late 1927, Wilder achieved fame and fortune beyond his wildest dreams. He resigned, for the last time, from Lawrenceville, settled in "the house *The Bridge* built" in Hamden, Connecticut, and pursued his career as a professional writer.

II   *Early Works: Expressions of Religious Humanism*

The best of Wilder's earliest dramatic writings were published in *The Angel That Troubled the Waters* (1928), a volume of sixteen three-minute plays selected from about forty he composed between 1915 and 1927. They prefigure the moral, religious, and esthetic themes and, to a certain extent, the style of his later works. While not without merit themselves, they are of interest chiefly because of the insights they offer into the humanistic and religious concerns that characterize Wilder's longer works and distinguish him from most of his contemporaries. He stated his intentions in the foreword to the book:

I hope, through many mistakes, to discover the spirit that is not unequal to the elevation of the great religious themes, yet which does not fall into repellent didacticism. Didacticism is an attempt at the coercion of another's free mind, even though one knows that in these matters beyond logic, beauty is the only persuasion. Here the schoolmaster enters. . . . He sees all that is fairest in the Christian tradition made repugnant to the new generations by reason of the diction in which it is expressed. The intermittent sincerity of generations of clergymen and teachers has rendered embarrassing and even ridiculous all the terms of the spiritual life. Nothing succeeds in damping the aspirations of the young today—who dares use the word "aspiration" without enclosing it, knowingly, in quotation marks?—like the names they hear given to them. The revival of religion is almost a matter of rhetoric. The work is difficult, perhaps impossible (perhaps all religions die out with the exhaustion of the language), but it at least reminds us that Our Lord asked us in His Work to be not only as gentle as doves, but as wise as serpents.

These plays—and most of his subsequent works—are attempts to bring fresh life and meaning to the "terms of the spiritual life." They are all parables or fables teaching Platonic or Christian lessons whose subjects include faith, love, humility, sacrifice, and the role and responsibility of the artist in society. The characters, for the most part two-dimensional, act upon one or another of these qualities—or upon superstition, reason, pride, or selfishness.

The first play in the volume, "Nascuntur Poetae," sets forth Wilder's Platonic theory of art. The Boy, who represents the unborn soul of the Poet, is shown being instructed in his responsibilities as an artist just prior to his birth into life from the world of eternal ideas. After being given the "gifts of pride and joy" by the Woman in the Chlamys, he is compelled by the Woman in Deep Red to accept "the dark and necessary gifts": a staff, for his journey through a life in which he will know no home; a crystal ball, which will enable him to see where other men cannot see, but which will forever deprive him of peace and satisfaction; and a chain, which will be a constant reminder of his obligations to his sacred calling and to his fellowmen. She says to him: "The life of man awaits you, the light laughter and the misery in the same day, in the selfsame hour the trivial and the divine. You are to give it voice. Among the bewildered and the stammering thousands you are to give it a voice and to mark its meaning."

This mystical, Platonic view of the writer and his purpose is found again in "Centaurs," where the romantic Shelley and the realist Ibsen are shown to have drawn the ideas for their works from the same transcendent source of eternal ideas, even though they used different forms and modes of presentation. Shelley expresses Wilder's conviction that "the stuff of which masterpieces are made drifts about the world waiting to be clothed in words. It is a truth that Plato would have understood that the mere language, the words of a masterpiece are the least of its offerings."

Platonism takes on a Christian cast in "Mozart and the Gray Steward." In this play, the Gray Steward (Death), assuming the role of an emissary from a nobleman, arrogantly offers Mozart a commission to write a requiem Mass for the nobleman's deceased wife. Mozart refuses, declaring that the nobleman and his wife are unworthy of his music. The Gray Steward then reveals his true self and accuses Mozart of failing in his obligation to "give a voice to all those millions sleeping, who have no one but you to speak for them." "Only through the intercession of great love," he tells Mozart, "and of great art which is love, can that despairing cry be eased." Christian humility becomes a moral responsibility for the artist when the Gray Steward, identifying the kingdom of art with the kingdom of heaven, warns Mozart that "only he who has kissed the leper can enter the kingdom of art."

Platonic and Christian mysticism conjoin in "And the Sea Shall Give up Its Dead," "Leviathan," and "Child Roland to the Dark Tower Came," in which the characters—dreading more than anything else the loss of their individuality—cling to their identity after death but lose all traces of self in the mystical "blaze of unicity" that is at once the realm of eternal ideas and the Mind of God. More directly and exclusively Christian are "Now the Servant's Name Was Malchus" and the last three plays in the volume, "Hast Thou Considered My Servant Job?" "The Flight into Egypt," and "The Angel That Troubled the Waters." These four plays have biblical characters and put forth Christian paradoxes.

In the first of these, the infinite mercy of Christ contends with and prevails over Satan's knowledge of human nature for the soul of the betrayer Judas. The title of this play is, of course, ironic and serves to accentuate the infiniteness of God's mercy through the contrast between the suffering servant Job and the traitor Judas. The theme of "The Flight into Egypt" is the discrepancy between faith and the facts of life. Indirectly, it is a gently satiric warning to believers that the attempt to rationalize faith is futile, that the real source of their faith is revelation, and that the best way to "prove" their faith is to live it. The donkey Hepzibah, who carries the Virgin Mary and the infant Jesus into Egypt, is the believer who insists on discussing with Mary the "matter of faith and reason." As Hepzibah discusses the question, she slows her pace and thus endangers her riders who symbolize the revealed justification for faith. When it occurs to her whom she is carrying, she admits that "it's a queer world where the survival of the Lord is dependent on donkeys, but it is so," and is advised by Mary to "do as I do and bear your master on."

In "The Angel That Troubled the Waters," the paradox of power-in-suffering arises from an action in which a man, a newcomer among the world's sufferers, asks the Angel who relieves sufferers to cure him of the impurity of his heart and his feelings of guilt so he can give his life to "Love's service"; that is, in service to mankind. The Angel refuses, saying: "It is your very remorse that makes your low voice tremble into the hearts of men. The very angels themselves cannot persuade the wretched and blundering children on earth as can one human being broken on the wheels of living. In Love's service only the wounded soldiers can serve."

Variations on the theme of the suffering servant of God—the Job theme—appear frequently in later works and so do variations on the Kierkegaardian theme of the absurd which appears in "Now the Servant's Name Was Malchus." In this play Malchus asks Our Lord to erase his name from the Book because people on earth have come to think of him as ridiculous because he had lost an ear to the sword of St. Peter while in the service of the High Priest. God replies that He too is ridiculous: "My promises were so vast that I am either divine or ridiculous. Malchus, will you stay and be ridiculous with me?" Like "The Flight into Egypt," this play contains a reminder of the faithful not to put too literal a construction on the Bible.

Each of these four plays is the work of a believer speaking primarily to other believers and cautioning them against intolerance, against trying to justify faith with reason, and against biblical literalism. They recall that faith is very difficult to maintain in the face of reason and the unpleasant facts of life—and that it is more often accompanied by suffering and doubt than by comfort and certitude.

The very conventionalism of such themes puts considerable burden upon the writer's power of give them fresh expression; and Wilder's extensive use of characters and materials from the cultural past instead of from life compounds this problem. But effective use of expressionistic techniques and of irony gives most of these plays remarkable vigor and novelty. Short as they are, they do develop and resolve conflicts. They build their tension dialectically, for the characters who embody ideas are pitted against one another. Most of the plays have, therefore, two main characters and a minor one. Usually the two main characters are moral protagonists: one holds conventional or superficial notions about such moral virtues as love, humility, and responsibility, about the role of art and the artist in life, or about religious faith and death; and the other, the stronger one, contends against these with ideas less soothing to human wishes, less intolerant, or less easily acceptable in terms of human pride or reason.

In "Fanny Otcott," for instance, a Bishop, grown "respectable" but feeling remorseful about an early stage career and a love affair with actress Fanny Otcott, calls upon her to announce that he intends to make a public confession of his youthful sins in order to clear his conscience of its burden of guilt. Fanny—a woman of questionable virtue by his recently acquired conventional concept of propriety—angrily denounces the greater immorality of his narrow moral orthodoxy. "You have borrowed your ideas from those who have never begun to live and who dare not," she tells him. Dedicated to life and the celebration of it in art, she refuses to make the love affair of their youth an immoral thing. She dismisses the Bishop, who has become spiritually attenuated by the binding restrictions of his creed, with: "Go away and tell your congregations what you please. I feel as though you were communicating to my mind some of those pitiable remorses that have weakened you. I have sinned, but I do not have that year [of our love affair] on my conscience. It is that year and my playing of Faizella that will bring troops of angels to welcome me to Paradise. Go away and tell your congregations what you please."

Looking back upon an artistic apprenticeship served in the writing of these plays, Wilder wrote in the foreword to *The Angel:* "The training for literature must be acquired by the artist alone, through the passionate assimilation of a few masterpieces written from a spirit somewhat like his own, and of a few masterpieces written from a spirit not at all like his own. I read all Newman and then I read all Swift. The technical processes of literature should be acquired almost unconsciously on the tide of a great enthusiasm, even syntax; even sentence-struction; I should like to hope, even spelling."

His more mature, longer stage plays would borrow less directly from the past than these playlets do, but would continue to examine the moral values of the Judeo-Christian tradition and employ models and materials derived from Classical Greek and Roman masterpieces. Wilder would also look elsewhere than to the prevailing realism and naturalism for modern models—to the theatrical expressionism of August Strindberg, for instance, rather than the social realism of Henric Ibsen or Henri Becque in the late nineteenth century, or the naturalism of Eugene O'Neill in his own time. The use of animated scenery in these three-minute plays, as well as characterizations that express or represent ideas, suggests that in addition to the Bible, Plato, and the Classical myths of Greece and Rome, he was "assimilating" the theatricalist modes of Strindberg's *Dream Play* and *Ghost Sonata.*

At times Wilder's nonrealism goes well beyond even Strindberg's and precludes enactment. This passage from "Hast Thou Considered My Servant Job?" for example, could hardly be staged: "Suddenly the thirty pieces of silver are cast upward from the revolted hand of Judas. They hurtle through the skies, flinging their enormous shadows across the stars and continue falling forever through the vast funnel of space." The only way to get the idea in the final clause across on stage would be to have it recited chorally, a narrative stage technique Wilder utilized extensively in such later plays as "Pullman Car Hiawatha," *Our Town*, and *The Alcestiad*, where a stage manager or another character addresses the audience directly about matters that cannot be satisfactorily expressed in action. There is, however, no chorus-person indicated for the three-minute plays and for that reason most of them could not be given full dramatic expression on stage. The problem of dramatizing abstractions and supernatural events without resorting to straight narrative was one that Wilder had to solve before he could satisfactorily stage the kind of nonrealistic plays he wanted to do.

Even though Wilder claimed he wrote some of these plays as late as 1927, when he was thirty, they are the finger-exercises of an apprentice writer experimenting with the devices of his craft. While several could be performed easily enough—and no doubt were by Thornton and his sisters—the action in many of them can be conveyed only through dialogue and stage directions and is intended to be perceived through mental images rather than performance. The author intended them to be read and grasped through the devices of poetry and rhetoric. Sprinkled with conceits, pathetic fallacies, and personifications common in the work of brilliant young writers, they reflect his attempts to achieve irony through parody or overstatement (and call to mind in this regard the juvenilia of Jane Austen and Emily Dickinson), balancing serious subjects or themes with wit or humor through manipulation of tone, diction, or mode. For instance, in "The Penny Beauty Spent," elevated dialogue is combined with the subjunctive mode to gain an ironic tone that modifies seriousness with comic hyperbole: "Even though all Versaille kill me with steel pins, Quinte shall have the watch." And in "The Message and Jehanne," a lofty, melodramatic tone prevents ponderousness when the present or perfect replaces the expected future tense: "It has broken my will. I am in flight for Padua. My family are nothing but sparrows."

Where the irony fails or is absent, the result is affectation, sentimentality, or didacticism, problems Wilder was never to be entirely free of; but in most instances the plays display a control of and an experimentation with language that suggest the emergence of a conscious stylist.

III   *The New Humanism*

Wilder's religious humanism, stylistic virtuosity, and technical versatility—observable in their beginning stages in *The Angel That Troubled the Waters*—were to become the hallmarks of his art. In combination they would distinguish his novels and plays from those of most of his contemporaries. More than most other novelists and playwrights of his generation, he was a product of the humanistic traditions promulgated by the liberal-arts schools and colleges, to which he remained close in temper as well as in physical proximity throughout his life; indeed, he often identified himself as a teacher first and a writer second. It was primarily in the universities that the "New Humanism," whose chief spokesmen were Irving Babbitt and Paul Elmer More, carried forward Matthew Arnold's nineteenth-century conflict with Darwinian apologist Thomas Henry Huxley, and challenged the assumptions and implications of philosophical naturalism. While Wilder's humanism differed in certain respects from that of the New Humanists, their basic beliefs concerning human nature and the value of the cultural past were his, and his works are best understood against the background of the intellectual dispute they—The New Humanists—were engaged in during the 1920s.

In retrospect, the battle of printed words that took place mainly during that decade seems to have been a teapot tempest whose long-term effects were minimal. Philosophical naturalists—literary as well as scientific—claimed that the Humanists stubbornly refused to accept the facts of life; they were accused in turn by the Humanists of having no sense of the past. Nevertheless, the debate went beyond accusations, helped redefine the bases of humanism and philosophical naturalism, and clarified the strengths and weaknesses of both positions.

The argument focused largely upon the nature of man and the degree to which human conduct is governed by instincts and environment, which the philosophical naturalists held to be paramount, or by an innate ethical sense, which the New Humanists argued raised humans above other animal species. While they did not deny that humans are a species of animal that, like other animals, is strongly influenced by its surroundings and passions, Babbitt and More (both of whom were professors of humanities) insisted that the "higher," moral nature of man distinguished him from other animals and provided him with the means to check his "lower," animal nature and respond to modes of conduct grounded in values.

Like its predecessors in fifth-century Greece and during the Renaissance, the New Humanism affirmed the dignity of man—when acting in moderation and according to the best of his inherited standards of thought and behavior—and rejected such "Demons of the Absolute"[4] as scientific rationalism, theories of progress, and Romantic idealization of the feelings as dangerous manifestations of human disproportion, or *hubris*. Reason and passion, head and heart, they believed, must be held in balance, and any improvement of the human lot, whether individual or collective, would have to be accomplished from within, morally, rather than from without, through changing the environment or reforming society. In these beliefs, the New Humanists were as much heirs of New England Puritanism as of the Classical and Renaissance past. For evidence of man's ethical aspirations, they cited the great masterpieces of literature and art of ancient Greece and Rome, the Renaissance, and the Judeo-Christian tradition which, they asserted, facilitate ethical perception through cultivation of the intuition (high imagination) and sensibility. By contrast, they deplored modern naturalistic works, such as those of Balzac, Zola, Maugham, Dreiser, and O'Neill, which portrayed humans as helpless pawns in a world of overwhelming, impersonal forces, and thus, they declared, debased humanity.

But while they were confronting philosophical naturalism on one front, they were attacked on another by critics who believed humanism could not stand without religious faith. T. S. Eliot posed the problem of what the final purpose of ethical conduct was to be in an essay published in 1927, "Humanism of Irving Babbitt,"[5] where he insisted that the ethical affirmations of the New Humanism could not subsist without religious justification; without it, Eliot concluded, man has no more reason to develop his ethical nature than to give way to his animal impulses.

More also came to recognize that humanism would ultimately have to look to religion for justification; for he rhetorically asked: "Will not the humanist, unless he adds to his creed the faith and hope of religion, find himself at the last, despite his protests, dragged back into the camp of the naturalist?" Eliot wrote: "Humanism is either an alternative to religion, or is ancillary to it . . . it always flourishes most when religion has been strong; and if you find examples of humanism which are anti-religious, or at least in opposition to the religious faith of the place and time, then such humanism is purely destructive, for it has never found anything to replace what it has destroyed." But on the other hand, Eliot added, "Any religion . . . is for ever in danger of petrifaction into mere ritual and habit, though ritual and habit be essential to religion. It is only renewed and refreshed by an awakening of feeling and fresh devotion, or by the critical reason. The latter may be the part of the humanist."

The New Humanism was a brief phenomenon that never quite became a movement. It lost its impetus in the 1930s when the more pressing economic and social issues of the Great Depression diminished interest in the academic and ethical questions they were concerned with. Babbitt and More and their allies, mostly from the universities, failed largely because they tried to make a philosophical doctrine from a broad, necessarily somewhat general body of assumptions about human nature and cultural values. They grounded their convictions too much upon a literary foundation, and their ethical interpretations of literature gave little attention to esthetic qualities.

Wilder's humanism was akin to the New Humanism in its insistence upon the validity of human values inherited from the cultural past, but his, like Eliot's, had a religious foundation and a sensitivity to the aesthetic as well as the ethical qualities of literature. Yet, unlike Eliot's, Wilder's Christian humanism was nondoctrinal and free of sectarian or ritualistic tendencies. Like Walt Whitman's it consisted of an attitude, a faith that life means something, and a conviction that all values must have the human individual at the center if they are to be worth anything. Whereas his humanism had a religious base to give it an ultimate jutification, it, by its very nature, held all dogmas and absolutes in suspension, and was as often directed against the excesses of religious belief and puritanical moralism as it was against the coldness of the rationalistic temper. In "Fanny Otcott," for instance, we see the Bishop's prudishness as a degradation of Fanny's commitment to life through love, and in the final four plays in *The Angel That Troubled the Waters* believers are warned against complacency and rationalism. Anything that bound the human spirit and prevented its freedom to love and create was the target of Wilder's critical humanism.

CHAPTER 2

Three Romance Novels

L IKE the plays in *The Angel That Troubled the Waters*, Wilder's first three novels—*The Cabala* (1926), *The Bridge of San Luis Rey* (1927), and *The Woman of Andros* (1930)—departed from the realism and philosophical naturalism that had dominated the drama since Ibsen and Becque and fiction since Zola and Howells. He was not alone in his departure, for by the 1920s nonrealistic movements were discernible in both genres. In the novel, Proust and Gide in France and Henry James in America had gone beyond the surface notations of literalist realism and the deterministic limitations of naturalism to a more subjective art based upon intuition. James combined psychological realism not only with fantasy in "The Turn of the Screw" but with symbolism in *The Wings of the Dove, The Sacred Fount,* and *The Golden Bowl;* Proust worked out a careful system of personal symbols in *Remembrance of Things Past;* and Gide was couching humanistic themes in such Classical vehicles as the Prometheus myth. All three dealt with moral and ethical themes that realistic, objective records of external phenomena could not convey and philosophical naturalism could not justify.

In the theatre, Strindberg had led the revolt against the realism of Ibsen in the latter part of the nineteenth century; and his influence was being felt in the expressionism of the German theatre in the 1920s. In Ireland, William Butler Yeats had tried poetic drama—of which *Cathleen ni Houlihan* was the best known—in the Abbey Theatre of Dublin. And in France Maurice Maeterlinck, Apollinaire, and Paul Claudel had rejected realism for symbolism, surrealism, and poetic religious drama, respectively.

The nonrealistic movement that had emerged by the 1920s was rich and varied; and it was to it that Wilder's work was allied. It is noticeable, however, that even in this era the main strength of the nonrealistic movement lay outside the United States where natu-

30

ralism and realism were securely established by Theodore Dreiser, Sinclair Lewis, and Eugene O'Neill and supported by the powerful pen of H. L. Mencken. Such excursions into expressionism as O'Neill's *Emperor Jones* (1920) and Elmer Rice's *The Adding Machine* (1923) and such deviations in romance as James Branch Cabell's *Jurgen* were exceptions rather than the rule. It is not surprising, then, that Wilder's works were regarded as radical departures from the literature of the day although they were part of a widespread, vigorous reaction to the realism of the latter part of the nineteenth century.

I   The Cabala

Edmund Wilson correctly observed that *The Cabala* reveals the influence of Proust[1] in the theme of the hopeless love of the person of superior sensibility (Alix) for one who is unworthy of it (Blair). But the influence of James Branch Cabell and Henry James is even greater than that of Proust. Like Cabell's esoteric romances, particularly *Jurgen*, *The Cabala* brings past and present together in modern and mythological characters but with this difference: Wilder brings his Classical gods to the present and suggests their presence in characters drawn with considerable realism; Cabell sends Jurgen back to the ages and places of the myths. The romantic re-creation of mythical characters typical of Cabell's work can be seen in Wilder's drawing of the Cabalists as modern incarnations of Jupiter (Cardinal Vaini), Demeter (Miss Grier), Pan (Marcantonio), Venus and Adonis (Alix and Blair), and Mercury (the narrator). Furthermore, *The Cabala* has an episodic structure unified by themes rather than by action in the manner of Cabell's *Chivalry*; but Wilder's episodes enjoy additional unity because the characters constitute a single group.

The influence of Henry James can be recognized in the general outline of the plot, in which an American cultural pilgrim goes to Europe with an admiring—at times naive and romantic—attitude toward it; meets a group of highly cultivated people by whom he is deeply impressed; and learns they are less than perfect but gains a new awareness of the cultural qualities his own country lacks. Like such famous Jamesian people as Mrs. Tristram of *The American*, Maria Gostrey of *The Ambassadors*, and Mrs. Stringham of *The Wings of the Dove*, Wilder's character is the interlocutor and the confidant whose dialogues with the principal characters define them and reveal the roots of their moral conflicts. He is also, in the manner of James's Strether in *The Ambassadors*, the "central intelligence" from whose point of view the narrative operates.

But while these similarities are palpable, Wilder's purposes are clearly not those of Cabell and James. Wilder shares Cabell's desire to use the materials of the Classical past in order to get beyond the limitations of literalist realism to the inner world of motives and desires. But where Cabell's characters typically search into the past for an ideal but end with a skeptical attitude to life, Wilder's narrator—likewise looking to the past for an ideal—carries forward into the future the spirit of the old tradition and accepts without disillusion the passing of the old order.

While it is apparent that Wilder was influenced by Cabell's non-realistic techniques, use of fantasy, stylistic grace, episodic structural arrangements, and romantic symbolism, his work is a refutation of a good deal of what Cabell said, especially in *Jurgen*. Wilder's soul-sick Marcantonio is a grim comment on the obsession with sex that pervades Cabell's work and his Alix is a reaffirmation of the higher, aristocratic qualities of an older order of womanhood that Cabell satirized. While Wilder, like Cabell, is concerned with the preservation of Hellenic-Christian culture, he affirms those humanistic principles of restraint and decorum that Cabell attacked, on their obverse side at least, as middle-class taboos.

Moreover, Wilder gives an ironic twist to the well-worn theme of the American abroad. Unlike most of James's people, Wilder's American gains from his European experience a new appreciation of the possibilities of culture in America. While he admires the European cultural tradition, he is not overwhelmed by it; and, when he returns to New York, he takes with him the conviction that a great culture is in the making in America and feels a sense of responsibility for bringing the best in the old culture to bear upon the new one. Such an attitude represents a departure not only from James but from most of Wilder's contemporaries in the "lost generation" as well; for most of them were still some years away from reconciliation with their homeland and some of them never became reconciled with it. The reconciliation in *The Cabala* arises from two dialectically developed conflicts: an historical conflict between past and present; and a moral conflict, growing out of the historical one, between the modernistic spirit of rationalism and materialism and the humanistic spirit of the past.

The main characters of *The Cabala* are a group of Roman

aristocrats whose misfortunes symbolize the decline of European culture. The action is reported by a young American scholar—whom the Cabalists call Samuele—who has become their confidant. Parallels between past and present run through the course of the narrative: a dying poet is a twentieth-century version of John Keats; the Cabalists are living in an ultramontane and royalist past; the spirit of Virgil pervades the scene and finally appears to the narrator as he departs for New York.

Living in the past, the Cabalists are in constant opposition with the forces of modernism. The conflict between past and present begins when the narrator, who has come to Rome to study the "ancients," finds them incarnate in the Cabala. While the moral themes develop during the course of five episodes and show the impact of the change in the social order upon the Cabalists, Samuele observes their fall and sees the decay of their admirable culture. In the second, third, and fourth episodes he sees the death of the old aristocratic order (as symbolized by Marcantonio); the impotence of the humane sensibility (Alix) before the indifferent, clinical probings of scholarship without the humanistic spirit (Samuele's fellow American scholar Blair); and the decline of the old vigorous Augustinian or Pauline faith (embodied by the Cardinal) in a Church that has lost touch with life. Finally, in the fifth chapter—when the young scholar-narrator invokes the spirit of Virgil and is told that "The secret is to make a city, not to rest in it"—he realizes that the past, whatever its glories, is dead and that his responsibility is to the present, the future, and America.

The three episodes that comprise chapters two, three, and four are moral tragedies in which Marcantonio, Alix, and Astree-Luce are victims of both their own anachronism and the modern rationalistic temper. Considering the shortness of the episodes, the chief characters are strikingly individual and their misfortunes deeply moving. The tragedy of the young nobleman Marcantonio, who commits suicide after an act of incest with his sister, is that—endowed with a passionate nature—he has no firm moral and religious code by which to discipline it and give it meaning and purpose. He symbolizes the decay of royalism and aristocracy. His death—like the mythical death of Pan, of whom he is the reincarnation—marks the end of a great period in history; for he is the only male heir the Cabalists have.

The events of the episode establish an impression of the inevitability of his death. Shortly after Samuele meets the Cabala,

Marcantonio's mother, the Duchess d'Aquilanera, asks him to help reform the boy, whose sex orgies are becoming a Roman scandal. Having found a suitable aristocratic marriage prospect for him, she wants Samuele to divert him from his debauchery until she can get him respectably married. Considerations of right and wrong in the boy's actions are not involved in her request; she is concerned solely with preventing his reputation from becoming so bad that the marriage will not materialize and the noble line from which he is descended be discontinued. Nor does the Cardinal, who also urges Samuele to help reform the boy for "a month or two," believe any longer in moral behavior. When Samuele accuses him of not really believing in temperance, he replies:

> Believe in it. Of course I do. Am I not a priest?
> Then why make the boy . . . ?
> But after all, *we are in the world.*
> I laughed. I shouted with a laughter that would have been insulting, if it hadn't contained a touch of hysteria. Oh, I thank thee, dear Father Vaini, I said to myself. I thank thee for that word. How clear it makes all Italy, all Europe. *Never try to do anything against the bent of human nature.* I came from a colony guided by exactly the opposite principle.

Marcantonio's moral corruption is an inevitable result of the decline of the ultramontane, aristocratic order into religious and political impotence. The dominant impression Wilder presents of the Cabalists is that, while they are all gifted in one way or another, they have fallen into uselessness; they retain the wealth, titles, social graces, and religious trappings of the aristocratic order without accepting its responsibilities. Robbed of their political and religious responsibilities, the Cabalists become morally decadent, weak-willed, and defenseless against the social forces that besiege them. Thus Marcantonio becomes hopelessly caught up in historical and moral conflicts he cannot contend with.

The network of forces, inner and outer, acting upon him gives this episode a remarkably complex and intense symbolic structure. The weight of a dead past is upon him in the obligations his title places upon him; the moral debility of the declining culture he represents makes him an easy prey to the moral nihilism of the modernistic international set whose standards he has adopted; Samuele's Puritan conscience, working upon his latent sense of guilt, ironically helps drive him to his final act of degradation and then suicide. The full tragic impact of Marcantonio's death is felt when his body is found by an officious American tourist, a Detroit manufacturer named Perkins, who has tried to use his acquaintance with Samuele as a pretext for an invitation to the Duchess' villa. Though he has been able to buy his way into Italy's most exclusive cultural sanctuaries, Perkins has not been able to penetrate the social screen that separates him from Italy's most exclusive families, the Cabalists. Failing to get an invitation from Samuele, he steals into the garden of the Villa, where he finds the body. The vulgarity of the American Philistine here provides a grim and ironic contrast to the fallen aristocratic greatness that Marcantonio symbolizes.

The moral decay that leads to Marcantonio's death is tied directly to the decline of religious faith, which is the theme of the episode involving Astree-Luce and the Cardinal. In this episode the clash between the simple, intuitive believer Astree-Luce and the Cardinal, who has lost his faith, results in a crushing loss of faith for her and an agonizing realization for him that he has committed an evil act. Wilder's humanist dialectic here sets the irrationalism of Astree-Luce in opposition to the rationalism of the Cardinal and resolves itself in a synthesis of enlightened faith and love. The Cardinal has lost his faith because, like his colleagues in the Vatican, he has lost touch with life. As a missionary in China he has been a great spiritual power, perhaps the greatest since St. Paul; but the relative isolation and orthodoxy of the Vatican have removed him from the real source of his faith: enactment of his moral principles in living. Deprived of contact with life, his principles have become an intellectual matter to him; and skepticism has won over faith.

Wilder's criticism here is directed not only at the petrifaction of religous orthodoxy—as represented by the "tiresome nonentites" in the Vatican who lack intellectual vigor—but at twentieth-century rationalism which has eaten away the Cardinal's faith and moral belief. The devitalized Church, concerned with matters of form and custom, is largely responsible for the moral and emotional deterioration of the Cardinal to whom faith has become an intellectual game. Detached from the intellectual and social currents of the day, the Church (standing for institutional religion in general) has lost its moral meaning for both Marcantonio and the Cardinal.

Yet the Cardinal himself is responsible for what he does to Astree-Luce to whom he is the greatest living man of faith. When he brings the full force of his great intellect upon her simple, naive faith, he becomes the epitome of evil; for he, misusing the power of his mind upon the feelings of one who lacks his endowment, has failed in his responsibility to those weaker than himself. The Cardinal is aware of the dangers of rationalism and the naturalistic spirit. When the narrator urges him, at the request of Astree-Luce, to write the great book she feels he can write, he refuses and condemns literature that reflects that spirit (Spengler, Frazer, Joyce, Proust, Freud) as "ordure." "What is the matter with this twentieth century of yours. . . ?" he demands. "You want me to compliment you because you have broken the atom and bent light? Well, I do, I do." But, ironically, it is that spirit that prompts him to crush Astree-Luce's faith.

Wilder's position is not anti-intellectual. Astree-Luce herself, the narrator declares, has always illustrated "the futility of goodness without intelligence." She is an intuitive believer, and while at times "she was able to let fall remarkable penetrating judgments," she is unequipped to deal with the Cardinal's rationalism, which, Samuele remarks, "would have had no effect on sound intellectual believers." The humanistic theme of enlightened faith—that is, the theme that religious faith must begin on the human level with love—arises when their relationship is rebuilt on a moral basis. The narrator comments: "When Astree-Luce and the Cardinal discovered that they were living in a world where such things could be forgiven, that no actions were too complicated but that love could understand, or dismiss them, on that day they began their lives all over again." This incident of the Cardinal and Astree-Luce is the most moving one in the book because both characters are deeply involved in the tragedy. The Cardinal, finally realizing the full implications of what he has done, reaches authentic tragic stature when, as an act of contrition, he embarks to resume his work in China but, falling mortally ill aboard ship, asks for burial at sea in order to erase any semblance of identity.

In the "Alix" episode the thematic unity of the book breaks down somewhat; but, next to the Cardinal, Alix is the most complex and compelling character in the book. In this episode the Princess Alix d'Espoli falls in love with Samuele's American scholar friend Blair, is coldly and rudely rejected by him, and suffers heartbreak and humiliation which bring to an end her friendship with Samuele as well as her affair with Blair. This theme, the Proustian one Edmund Wilson has called it,[2] of the agonizing love of a superior person (Alix) for an inferior one, is the central one of the episode; but while there is agonized suffering in the other episodes, this one differs from them because the suffering does not carry with it the concept of cultural decline. That this theme was intended for this chapter is indicated in the beginning when the narrator lists the activities of the Cabala after the death of Marcantonio. These consist of stirring up public opinion about the "faint smell of drains" in the Vatican; sending to Berlin for a tree doctor to save some oaks in the Borghese Gardens; and blocking the advancement in the Church of "several tiresome nonentities." "To tell the truth," Samuele remarks, "their accomplishments were not very considerable. I soon saw that I had arrived on the scene in the middle of the decline of their power." Having tried to deal with matters of greater import in Italy and failed, "they realized that the century had let loose influences they could not stem, and contented themselves with less pretentious assignments."

But the cultural decline is not realized in the main episode itself. Alix, herself, symbolizes the best of the old aristocratic tradition. She "is not really modern"; in her one may "glimpse into the seventeenth century and . . . reconstruct . . . what the aristocratic system must have been like in its flower." However, Blair does not represent anything peculiarly modern, so only half of the past-present conflict is found in the chapter. The tension at the center of the episode is that between sensibility and intellect; and only the former is connected (but *both* are in the following chapter) with the past-present conflict.

Alix, a sort of Jamesian character, is a woman of excellent qualities who is ill equipped to contend with the vagaries of natures not her equal. Most of the third chapter is given to the demonstration of her excellence and to the suggestion of a relationship between a character such as hers and a work of art, a parallel faintly suggestive of James's picture of Milly Theale in *The Wings of the Dove*. Alix is the mime, the artist, who needs the active participation of an audience for the success of her social talents. She has a wound-and-bow talent that flourishes under suffering; and she is most witty and entertaining when her suffering is most intense. Her highly developed sensibility and her wit make her the delight of all—except Blair—who know her.

Blair does not recognize—or does not appreciate—her talents and virtues; and her humiliation at being seen by Blair and Samuele at a séance is the final, crushing blow to her pathetically desperate attempts to find an outlet of some sort for her great spiritual resources. Because of her choice, superstition triumphs over her native intelligence and a balanced sensibility is thrown out of balance. Her profound need for love is never satisfied, and her "exquisite" nature breaks in the presence of Blair's cold intellectualism. This development is the purport of the third chapter.

The moral theme of love is satisfactorily carried by the action, as is the symbolic significance of the dissociation of intellect and sensibility; but the intended tension between time past and time present fails to evolve, and the chapter lacks that important relationship with the others. Despite this defect, the character of Alix is so compellingly drawn that the breakdown in unity tends to be forgotten in reading the chapter. Although there is a good measure of sentimentalism in the drawing of Alix, she stands in the tradition of the Jamesian heroine and does credit to it.

Wilder's attempt to weave together the conflicts between past and present and between traditional moral values and such naturalistic by-products as rationalism, skepticism, and hedonism is only partly successful in *The Cabala*. In addition to the fact that the historical theme is not adequately developed in the Alix episode, there are other violations of unity—most notable of which are a digression about the family history of the American Miss Grier and a portrait of the German Mrs. Bernstein, neither of which contributes to the action or themes in any way. Nor are the realism and fantasy brought together in an entirely satisfactory manner. The book begins realistically and the characters and incidents are developed throughout with such compelling realism as individuals that Miss Grier's claim, near the end of the book, that they are the Olympian gods incarnate seems arbitrary and contrived, an unconvincing alteration of the Cabalists from symbols of the past to literal embodiments of it. The intent of Miss Grier's explanation and of the invocation of Virgil is to make explicit the theme that the spirit of the past is alive. But this theme has already been suggested in the symbolic development of the chief characters, and the sudden shift to fantasy and explicit statement reduces the effectiveness of the irony in the simultaneous buildup of the Cabalists as sharply defined individuals and symbols.

Yet from the standpoint of character development this is a remarkable first novel. Each of the main characters is highly complex and vital, and the episodes dealing with them as individuals have the stamp of authenticity. *The Bridge of San Luis Rey* shows a substantial improvement in Wilder's technical skill, but the characters in *The Cabala* are as powerful and as memorable as any in *The Bridge*.

II   The Bridge of San Luis Rey

Like *The Cabala, The Bridge of San Luis Rey* (1927) is a romance. Although the fantasy of *The Cabala* is missing, *The Bridge* has the remoteness of setting, the symbolism, the yoking together of past and present, the moral and religious themes, and the episodic structure of the earlier book; and in it Wilder attempts, as he did in *The Cabala*, to capture not only surface realism but the complex workings of the inner life as well. He had stated his conviction that the purely realistic fiction of the day had run the course of its usefulness and effectiveness when he told Harry Salpeter in 1928 that he felt that America was turning away from the rule of realism to the introspective novel. "Until about ten years ago," he told Salpeter, "experience was very valuable as a preparation toward the writing of novels. Authors who had been stokers and barhands did bring something valuable to America in the process of discovering itself. But now the notation of things has been done so well through such men as Sinclair Lewis that from now on the profounder assimilation of a little experience rather than a rapid view of a great deal is the more desirable. Literature, now that America has discovered itself, could spring from solitude and reflection, with less emphasis on observation and more on intuition."[3]

Nevertheless, in both *The Cabala* and *The Bridge* the characters are portrayed with considerable realism and clarity as individuals; and, from the standpoint of response to the promptings of the flesh and susceptibility to forces of environment and heredity, they are conceived with enough naturalism to allay any charges that Wilder ignores the observable and unpleasant facts of life. Marcantonio's losing struggle with his "lower nature," for instance, is as compulsive as, and has a pathetic consequence similar to, that of Clyde Griffith in Dreiser's naturalistic *American Tragedy;* and Camila Perichole in *The Bridge* feels the same physical attraction to bullfighters that Hemingway's Lady Brett Ashley does in *The Sun Also Rises*. The Cabalists and the victims of the disaster at San Luis Rey, moreover, are as subject to the forces of history and circumstance as any characters of Dos Passos or Stephen Crane.

But Wilder's humanism precludes what he regards as the onesidedness of philosophical naturalism and realism. The characteristic feature of these two novels and of *The Woman of Andros* is the inclusion of the inner as well as the outer facts of life with the intent of reaffirming the sense of the mystery of life which

realistic and naturalistic writers had tended to ignore in their concern with external, observable data and with the power of heredity
and environment. Wilder gives full scope to the claims of scientific,
observable, objective knowledge (as manifested in literature by
naturalism); but he insists that the inner life—the passions, the intellect, the hopes and the aspirations—is a mystery whose workings
and purposes defy rationalization. The life of the mind is one of
constant struggle between the lower and the higher qualities in
man. Moreover, that inner struggle has a metaphysical parallel in
the universal tension between chance and purpose. This view of
course is not original, but the achievement of it in a literary work is
difficult. If the work is original, the ideas take on fresh meaning.

Wilder revealed that it had been his intention in these early
works to try to restore the aura of mystery to life when he told
Walther Tritsch in a Berlin interview in 1931 that "It is the magic
unity of purpose and chance, of destiny and accident, that I have
tried to describe in my books."[4] The superiority of *The Bridge* over
The Cabala consists in large part in its more successful achievement
of the "magic unity" through dialectic. The action of *The Bridge*
begins when Brother Juniper, a Franciscan monk, sees the bridge
fall and the five victims plunge to their deaths in the canyon below.
"Why did this happen to *those* five?" he asks. "If there were any
plan in the universe at all, if there were any pattern in a human life,
surely it could be discovered mysteriously latent in those lives so
suddenly cut off. Either we live by accident and die by accident, or
we live by plan and die by plan."

Convinced the incident is an act of God, he sees in it an opportunity to observe God's intentions "in a pure state"; but, when his
investigation of the lives of the victims shows no pattern of cause
and effect, he concludes that the "discrepancy between faith and
the facts is greater than is generally assumed." Juniper's mistake is
that he never learned the "central passion" of the lives of the three
adult victims—the Marquesa de Montamayor, Pio, and Esteban. So
the omniscient author steps in to recount these intimate facts,
although he admits that it is "possible that even I have missed the
very spring within the spring." We move, then, from the extrinsic
motivations revealed by Juniper's investigation to the intrinsic
motivations in the minds and hearts of the victims.[5]

Wilder borrowed some of his material for *The Bridge* from
Prosper Mérimée's *La Carosse Du Saint Sacrement*. In the
Perichole, he combined Mérimée's Perichole with the parrot that

taunts her; and he drew the Marquesa de Montemayor after Mérimée's marquise d'Altamire.[6] But it is with Conrad's *Chance*, rather than Mérimée's work, that the book can most profitably be compared. Like *Chance*, *The Bridge* explores the themes of moral isolation and love and raises the question of whether events occur by accident or design. The title of Conrad's novel is ironic: life is not a matter of chance or accident.[7] Even where chance appears to govern men's lives—as it does in the events involving Flora de Barral and young Powell—there are causal factors at work. Conrad took as the epigraph for *Chance* a quotation from Sir Thomas Browne: "Those who hold that all things are governed by fortune had not erred, had they not persisted there." While Browne believed that all events have a divine cause, Conrad showed them in *Chance* to be governed by human motivation. He presented a series of incidents that seemed to be the result of sheer chance, but then showed that behind the appearance of accident was an intricate network of human causes. Flora's suicide attempt, for instance, appears to have been caused by a chain of misfortunes that began with her father's financial disaster; but it actually can be explained by her abusive treatment at the hands of the disgruntled Eliza, whose actions can also be explained in terms of clear-cut traits of character.

Wilder's strategy is to set forth the two alternatives by means of external and internal evidence—that which Brother Juniper adduces to prove the presence of the hand of God in the fall of the bridge, and that which he cannot see because it is in the minds and hearts of the characters. Juniper combines the two extreme and dogmatic interpretations of the incident: the scientific, which sees the fall as something that can be explained in physical terms; and the orthodox Christian, which sees in all events the operation of Providence. Both of these views are based upon externals, and Juniper's collection of data in the scientific manner in order to settle a theological question is a *reductio ad absurdum* of both positions, since his investigations lead to no conclusion at all.

Attention is thus directed to the inner sources of evidence when the omniscient author points to the "central passion" in each of the major characters. Beyond this purely human explanation lies the suggestion that there is a divine cause in the "central passion," love, in the victims. The fall of the bridge of San Luis Rey symbolizes the force of circumstance or of the meaningless workings of nature, but the passions of the victims act as the primary human cause leading them to the bridge. Fusion of these two factors brings about the "magic unity" of purpose and chance that provides the element of mystery which is the essence of mysticism. The applicability of the Browne epigraph to *The Bridge* is thus apparent: those who hold that the fall of the bridge was an accident would not err in their position if they did not insist upon its being the whole truth. To this Wilder adds: those who believe would not err if they did not insist, as Juniper does, upon proving God's presence in all the events of life.

Between the first chapter ("Perhaps an Accident") and the last ("Perhaps an Intention"), three flashback chapters recount the lives of the three chief victims up to the time of the disaster. Each of them, it turns out, is a person with deep spiritual attachments whose "central passion" is thwarted either by emotional coldness or selfishness or by natural circumstance. But each is also governed to such an extent by his consuming passion that the conflict it generates and the disaster that follows it have the earmarks of fate. Yet each one is a free spirit and has an opportunity, just before the fall of the bridge, to make a compromise with the circumstances of his situation and rebuild his moral life. The vision is a tragic one. Their deaths are an inescapable fact, regardless of the interpretation one makes of their lives; but their deaths are not entirely futile, since they generate a love in the survivors that did not exist before.

The sense of mystery is achieved in the episodes dealing with the individual victims, whose complexity demonstrates why Juniper's investigation is futile. The Marquesa de Montemayor has fixed her whole spiritual being upon her daughter, Dona Clara, who has married a Spanish nobleman to escape her mother's extreme affection. Cold and intellectual like her father (and like Blair in *The Cabala*), Dona Clara is the opposite of the Marquesa, whose love for her daughter is the chief factor in her life. Dona Clara sails from Peru to Spain "with the most admirable composure, leaving her mother to gaze after the bright ship, her hand pressing now her heart and now her mouth."

The object of her life gone, the Marquesa turns in upon herself and lives a mental drama in which she and her daughter live as she, the Marquesa, would have them live. "On that stage were performed endless dialogues with her daughter, impossible reconciliations, scenes eternally recommenced of remorse and forgiveness," the Marquesa always being the one who forgave and the daughter feeling remorse. To the people of Lima there was no indication that the Marquesa was suffering the agonies of the unloved. They knew her as a slovenly, drunken old woman who talked to herself; at one time there was a petition circulated to have her locked up, and she had been denounced by the Inquisition. They were unaware, when interviewed by Juniper, that she read widely and that she wrote letters to her daughter (letters Wilder patterned after those of Madame de Sévigné) which "in an astonishing world have become the textbook of schoolboys and the anthill of grammarians." These letters, like all great literature, reflected "the notation of the heart."

But while genius was concealed by outward ugliness and kindled by suffering, the Marquesa had moral weaknesses that were a part of the love that generated the great letters. For one thing, her devotion to her daughter was "not without a shade of tyranny: she loved her daughter not for her daughter's sake, but for her own." And even the great letters, in their sophisticated tone of detached amusement at the people and events in Lima, concealed the lack of humility and courage in the love that produced them. The Marquesa learns the lessons of humility and courage from the orphan girl Pepita, who also dies in the disaster.

Pepita, whose devotion to the Abbess, Madre Maria, is as strong as the Marquesa's for Dona Clara, is sent by the Abbess to serve the Marquesa. Feeling as strongly about her separation from the Abbess as the Marquesa does about hers from her daughter, Pepita writes a letter to the Abbess asking to return to the convent. She does not send the letter, however, because she feels it "wasn't brave." The Marquesa, having read the letter, discovers in it the humility and willingness to sacrifice that she herself lacks. The night before the fall of the bridge, watching Pepita as she sleeps, the Marquesa whispers to herself, "Let me live now . . . Let me begin again."

The Marquesa's "central passion" gains an added dimension by her apparent victory over circumstance. Like Pepita, she has had an unfortunate beginning in life, Pepita being an orphan, the Marquesa having had an unhappy childhood. Pepita, however, since coming under the guardianship of the Abbess, has lived in an atmosphere of love and sacrifice that has enabled her to withstand the affliction of separation with courage, which the Marquesa was not able to do without losing her religion and seeking escape in drinking. The Marquesa's life has been directed by circumstance up to the time she reads Pepita's letter, since, in addition to having a daughter who is cold toward her, her selfishness and lack of courage

both stem from an unhappy childhood and a marriage she was forced into against her will. When she decides to "begin again,"
therefore, she affirms the triumph of her will over circumstance.
Yet, ironically, she seems to lose to circumstance finally when the
bridge falls.

The complex development of the Marquesa's character and the
interplay between the forces of will and circumstance preclude any
easy metaphysical or theological affirmations. The episode ends in
mystery, as do those involving Esteban and Pio. But the moral imperative of love is clear enough; and the highest love is the kind of
disinterested love shown by Pepita and by the Abbess, whose life is
devoted to the care of the suffering. The levels of love are worked
out in a somewhat broader fashion in the Esteban chapter and
represent Wilder's humanistic answer to the contention that love is
a purely human contrivance.

At the lowest level are Camila's shabby, clandestine affairs with
various men of Lima. She hires Manuel to write letters to her lovers,
all of whom she quarrels with and almost casually abandons. In contrast to her animal-like passion, vulgarity, and absence of profound
feeling is Manuel's brief but intense love for her. Manuel himself is
not inexperienced sexually; for both he and Esteban "had possessed
women, and often, especially during their years at the waterfront;
but simply, Latinly." His love for Camila, however, represents a
departure from purely physical pleasure: ". . . it was the first time
that his will and imagination had been thus overwhelmed." That is,
he rose for the first time to a human level in love and above the
mere promptings of nature. He "had lost that privilege of simple
nature, the dissociation of love and pleasure." Understanding
nothing higher than physical pleasure, Camila is cynical about love.
"There is no such thing as that kind of love," she tells Pio. "It's in
the theater you find such things." But Manuel, without art or learning, has no such cynicism. Love is as natural to him as pleasure, but
more intense, and in it one undergoes a "crazy loss of one's self."
He represents an affirmation that love may spring from a higher
source than sexual desire.

He shows an even higher type of love than this love for Camila in
giving her up for the sake of Esteban. Again, there is no intellectual
analysis, no reflection, in his sacrifice. He intuitively feels the isolation of Esteban; and, while his attachment to him is not so complete
as Esteban's for him, it is strong enough to make Manuel willing to
sacrifice to save his brother from misery.

Yet profound as Manuel's devotion to Esteban is, it falls below Esteban's for him. If Manuel's love is characterized by sacrifice, Esteban's is characterized, after Manuel's death by blood poisoning, by the complete identity of himself with his brother. But Esteban discovers in Manuel's attraction to Camila "that secret from which one never quite recovers, that even in the most perfect love one person loves less profoundly than the other. There may be two equally good, equally beautiful, but there may never be two that love one another equally well." Esteban's love attains the level of the tragic, for it is a part of the human condition that "the most perfect love" is never quite perfect.

This ascending scale of types of love, culminating in Esteban's devotion to his brother, sets the stage for Captain Alvarado, who has also suffered a loss, that of a daughter. The cause of the girl's death is not mentioned, but it is implied that there is no more "reason" for it than for Manuel's. The captain's grief is as profound as Esteban's, but they react in opposite ways. The captain travels "about the hemispheres," as the Marquesa writes to Dona Clara, "to pass the time between now and his old age." Yet he is reconciled to life, is determined to live it out to its end, and even hopes to see the girl again. Esteban cannot, however, face life or reconcile himself to it without Manuel. His identification with Manuel is so complete that he buries himself, figuratively, and assumes Manuel's name; and the night before the bridge falls, he attempts suicide. The inability of Esteban to face life without his brother symbolizes the pathos of man before circumstance. Endowed with a profound capacity for love and for pain, Esteban is unable either to comprehend or to accept a world which cares for neither. When the captain asks him to sail aboard his ship, he accepts in the hope that he can escape from his hopelessness in ceaseless activity. But this hope is short-lived: he cannot leave Peru, where Manuel is buried.

By the end of the Esteban episode, the moral qualities that comprise the highest form of human love appear in the acts of courage, humility, and sacrifice performed by the victims prior to the fall of the bridge. In the Pio episode, love is seen in terms of its highest and most concrete expression in art. The theme of artistic beauty being wrested from ugliness through the agency of love, a minor theme in the Marquesa episode, is developed fully in the Pio chapter. When Pio decides to "play Pygmalion" with Camila, his three great passions—"his passion for overseeing the lives of others, his worship of beautiful women, and his admiration for the treasures

of Spanish literature"—assume moral significance. Until he meets
Camila, Pio is totally unscrupulous. The conflict that develops when
he begins to train her for the stage is the conflict between the artist
(it is he, more than Camila, who is the artist) and his recalcitrant
materials, the raw life from which the artist creates. Camila is Pio's
"great secret and reason for his life"; but she is "quite incapable of
establishing any harmony between the claims of her art, of her
appetites, of her dreams, and of her crowded daily routine." Each of
these is "a world in itself, and the warfare between them would
soon have reduced to idiocy (or triviality) a less tenacious phy-
sique." Lack of a profound love to integrate the various claims upon
her leaves Camila without any real meaning in her life. She lives
almost at random, the theatre at times capturing her enthusiasm,
love at others; but nothing lasts for long, including her love for the
Viceroy, whose mistress she becomes. Once during the twenty years
she and Pio are associated love comes into her life—when she first
meets the Viceroy—and then her acting reaches its perfection.

Pio's attempts to bring art and life together in a perfect union in
Camila are successful only when love is present to bridge the gap
between the two, yet the love that informs both is accompanied by
suffering. This profoundest love, Pio believes, is a "cruel malady
through which the elect are required to pass in their late youth and
from which they emerge, pale and wrung, but ready for the
business of living." He has the humility and compassion that come
from the "illness" of love—the "rich wisdom" of the heart that
Camila does not find until she has lost her beauty (by smallpox),
Pio, and her son Jaime.

Having thus defined love and the abstract qualities that give it
moral significance, Wilder concludes the book with the theme of
love as a moral responsibility. All the survivors realize their failure
to respond to the love directed toward them, imperfect though it
was in the cases of Pio and the Marquesa. The full impact of love as
a first condition to meaningful living comes to all the survivors after
the disaster; and the Abbess, the only character in the book whose
life has fulfilled itself in love (although even she, as she confesses to
herself, has been too busy to appreciate fully the devotion of Pepita)
expresses the significance of love in a world meaningless and pur-
poseless with it: "Even now . . . almost no one remembers Esteban
and Pepita, but myself. Camila alone remembers her Uncle Pio and
her son; this woman [Dona Clara], her mother. But soon we shall
die and all memory of those five will have left the earth, and we

ourselves shall be loved for a while and forgotten. But the love will have been enough; all those impulses of love return to the love that made them. Even memory is not necessary for love. There is a land of the living and a land of the dead and the bridge is love, the only survival, the only meaning."

Limited as it is to the human level, this proposition is directed to believers and skeptics alike; it warns both that, whatever their beliefs about God, love is indispensable if life is to have any meaning. The question raised by Juniper remains a mystery; the "perhapses" in the titles of the first and last chapters remain. At one level, human motivation brought the victims to the bridge at the same time—and in this *The Bridge* resembles *Chance*—but these motives have been shown to be so bound up with circumstance that the two are hardly separable. Moreover, as Juniper's investigation shows, the "good" died with the "bad"; there was no discernible relationship between desert and reward. Moral behavior, Wilder maintains, is, therefore, a purely human responsibility and has clear-cut human consequences. Whatever the interpretation of the disaster, it generated in the survivors a love that had not previously existed.

The theological and metaphysical question remains, however, in the "magic unity" achieved in the mysterious synthesis of circumstance and human motivation; and the sense of mystery in the lives and deaths of the characters provides an option for both believer and nonbeliever; at the same time the mysterious is in itself, paradoxically, the basis for a mystical interpretation. With regard to the persuasive effect of "magic unity"—which it was Wilder's declared aim to achieve—Kenneth Burke has remarked: "Mystery is a major resource of persuasion. Endow a person, an institution, a thing with the glow or resonance of the Mystical, and you have set up a motivational appeal to which people spontaneously ('instinctively,' 'intuitively') respond. In this respect, an ounce of 'Mystery' is worth a ton of argument."[8] This mystery in the lives of the characters convinces rather than the "arguments" set against one another by Juniper. Thus, while Wilder doesn't say it in *The Bridge*, the "spring within the spring"—the love that bridges the land of the living and the land of the dead—has mystical significance.

The Bridge has often been charged with being sentimental, but there are really no grounds for such a charge because Wilder gives full enough scope to the weaknesses of the characters to preclude the expenditure of any undue feeling for them. Furthermore, there are no tears of happiness at the end of their suffering; their love in each case brings pain, and, finally, death. Nor is the book so optimistic as it might seem to be at first reading.

Yet *The Bridge* is not an unqualified success as a novel. Its most noticeable weakness is the episodic structure which, though thematically unified, obviates progression in a single narrative line. Characters are developed in one episode only to be dropped almost entirely in the next one and replaced by a new cast. Another weakness—its most important technical one—is the sometimes obtrusive presence of the omniscient author, who judges and interprets as he narrates the histories and inner lives of the main characters. This subjective, arbitrary narration weakens the dramatic structure of the book, although it is compensated for to a considerable degree by the fact that the dramatic scenes embody or suggest much of what the omniscient author says about the characters. Wilder was aware of the defects of omniscient author narration and came to favor the stage over the novel as an art form partly because he was convinced that dramatic narration eliminates the subjective presentation that he felt was inherent to the novel.

Still, there is a strong dramatic quality to *The Bridge;* and the proclivity for direct, objective presentation that was to lead Wilder to turn his attention in the 1930s primarily to playwrighting can be seen in such passages as the following where the character of Pio, the loving but obsessed perfectionist taskmaster, comes through—as does the imperious, cruel but childlike nature of Camila—in dialogue and shortview narrative:

At the close of a performance Camila would return to her dressing room to find Uncle Pio whistling nonchalantly in one corner. She would divine his attitude at once and cry angrily:
"Now what is it? Mother of God, Mother of God, what is it now?"
"Nothing, little pearl. My little Camila of Camilas, nothing."
"There was something you didn't like. Ugly fault-finding thing that you are. Come on now, what is it? Look, I'm ready."
"No, little fish. Adorable morning star, I suppose you did as well as you could."
The suggestion that she was a limited artist and that certain felicities would be forever closed to her never failed to make Camila frantic. She would burst into tears:
"I wish I had never known you. You poison my whole life. You just think I did badly. It pleases you to pretend that I was bad. All right then, be quiet."

Uncle Pio went on whistling.

"The fact is I know I was weak tonight, and don't need you to tell me so. So there. Now go away. I don't want you around. It's hard enough to play that part without coming back and finding you this way."

Suddenly Uncle Pio would lean forward and ask with angry intensity, "Why did you take that speech to the prisoner so fast?"

More tears from the Perichole: "Oh, God, let me die in peace! One day you tell me to go faster and another to go slower. Anyway I shall be crazy in a year or two and then it won't matter."

More whistling.

Each of Pio's passions is manifest in these lines: "his passion for overseeing the lives of others, his worship of beautiful women, and his admiration for the treasures of Spanish literature," which Camila was enacting. And Camila's sloth, her vulgar arrogance, but withal her driving obsession for perfection and her despair at not achieving it, and the hint that her exasperation will lead her finally to less arduous pursuits—all are found in this dialogue.

The Bridge has continued to hold its place high among the distinguished company of novels written during the 1920s by such men as Lewis, Hemingway, Fitzgerald, and Dos Passos—different as it is from their works. Despite its technical weaknesses, it has all the intellectual scope, depth of feeling, and complexity of character that make a mature and aesthetically satisfying vision. It was an unusual, courageous act in the twenties for a serious writer to affirm the moral nature and value of love—a subject most serious writers were associating in one way or another with sex. The almost inherently banal and sentimental "higher" manifestations of love were being abandoned to the hack writers or rejected as "genteel." But as he defines love in *The Bridge*, it is a most difficult thing; for it is accompanied by selfishness, confronted by human coldness, and lost upon a universe that does not seem to know or care that it exists. Considering the critical climate that prevailed in the twenties, it might fairly be said of Wilder himself what he says in *The Bridge:* "There are times when it requires high courage to speak the banal." In *The Bridge*, the familiar takes on new life and meaning in art.

III   The Woman of Andros

The Cabala took place in Rome, 1920; *The Bridge* in Peru, 1714; and Wilder's third novel, *The Woman of Andros*, went farther back in time and place to pre-Christian Greece. Published in 1930, *The Woman* appeared at an unpropitious time, for the depression was under way and the climate of opinion was not favorable to fiction that ignored current economic and political problems. Understandably, the book failed with both the critics and the public.

The depression was not the only factor contributing to its failure; it had its own serious defects. Wilder was becoming increasingly derivative as he went back in time. In *The Bridge* he gave the material he borrowed from Mérimée the flavor of his own developing narrative genius, but in *The Woman* he reverted to the aestheticism and "poetic" style that characterized the three-minute plays and to the subjective mode of presentation that had marred the generally objective presentation of *The Cabala* and *The Bridge*. Furthermore, the irony that brought complexity to the earlier novels was absent from *The Woman*, as was the element of dramatic realism which gave the themes of these books concrete embodiment and integration in action. Operating on two thematic levels, the moral and the historical, *The Woman* did not successfully weave those themes together. The historical theme, represented by the coming of Christ, was thrust into the story arbitrarily at the beginning and the end.

Of course the book is not the failure this list of weaknesses makes it appear to be. If it lacks the dramatic intensity of the other works, it has the virtues as well as the infirmities of that poetic, nonrealistic side of Wilder which distinguished him from most of his contemporaries. But as is true with most important writers, his artistic virtues and vices are closely allied—and Wilder's vices generally are his virtues in excess; in *The Woman* the author's skill in fine writing draws undue attention to itself. The concise and evocative qualities of his style, for instance, are present; but they descend at times into sententiousness and, on occasion, into preciousness.

The Woman is Wilder's most direct attempt in a novel to show the religious propensities of the Classical Greek humanistic temper. The first part of the book is based upon Terance's comedy, *The Andria*, which in turn was based upon two lost plays of Menander. A short book, *The Woman* is a simple story involving many of the same characters of the Terence original: a Greek boy Pamphilus, his father Simo, the hetaera Chrysis (the "woman"), and her younger sister Glycerium. Wilder left out, however, such of Terence's characters as Davus, Charinus, and Dromo; and he altered the story to suit his own religious-humanistic purposes. His Glycerium, for example, is really the sister of Chrysis; Terence's only pretends to be and is actually the daughter of the merchant Chremes. Also,

Wilder does not solve Pamphilus' problem, as Terence did, by having it discovered that the pregnant Glycerium is the daughter of Chremes. Nor is there a *homo ex machina* such as Crito to save the day. Wilder's Pamphilus has to face the facts that Glycerium is the sister of a hetaera and that she is pregnant. And, finally, Wilder's Glycerium dies, as Terence's does not. As these changes indicate, Wilder made a serious novel out of Terence's comedy.

But while he discarded the love affair of Charinus and Philumena, Wilder retained the Terentian "double plot" by placing beside the love affair of Pamphilus and Glycerium the conflict between the humanistic Chrysis and the "respectable," conventional citizens of Brynos. Chrysis symbolizes the spirit of Classical Greek culture; she is Socratic (and, in fact, quotes Socrates at length) in her approach to life, in her spirit of inquiry, and in her having a group of young disciples. Like Socrates, she is at odds with society; but, being an outcast and unconfused and uncomplicated by social conventions, she is able to live and observe life in its pure state. With her, Pamphilus—her most intelligent but least vocal disciple—is looking for the meaning of life.

Along with a Captain Philocles (who, like Captain Alvarado in *The Bridge*, has lost a daughter and is "filling the hours in anticipation of release from a life that had lost its savor"), they find that only when they have "died to themselves" and thus rid themselves of "that self that supports the generality of men, the self that is a bundle of self-assertations, of greeds, of vanities, and of easily offended pride," can they begin really to live. Chrysis' home is a rufuge for the oppressed and the weak—all who suffer. Like the Abbess in *The Bridge*, she finds that life means nothing except what self-sacrifice and love impose upon it. But she is pre-Christian, and there is no higher justification or sanction for her higher impulses. "Someday," she says, "we shall understand why we suffer. I shall be among the shades underground and some wonderful hand, some Alcestis, will touch me and will show me the meaning of all these things. . . ." The source of suffering is shown here, as in *The Bridge*, to lie in the conflict between external circumstance and self-preoccupation on the one hand and the internal world of "love, virtue, and wisdom," which only a very few people cultivate, on the other. The tragedy of life consists in the realization that one is failing in the latter. Chrysis finds that it is "true, true beyond a doubt, tragically true, that the world of love and virtue and wisdom [is] the true world and her failure in it all the more overwhelming."

Chrysis represents the Classical humanistic spirit attempting to translate its ideals into action and searching for a final justification in religion for its values. When she dies, she is concerned lest she die like an animal rather than a human being. Her humanity has come from the culture of fifth-century Greece which above all affirmed human dignity; and her greatest concern is to retain that dignity even in the face of death. Although her values lack divine sanction until the birth of Christ, Chrysis yearns for higher justification for her moral principles: "If only the gods were sometimes among us. To have nothing to go by except this idea, this vague idea, that there lies the principle of living." But she dies before the coming of Christ, which, we are told in the first and final paragraphs of the book, is shortly to occur.

Malcolm Cowley has rightly called *The Woman* a Greek pastoral. Its heightened diction, quiet tone, and spare, classical structure give it the qualities of a narrative poem. Almost in the manner of a pastoral elegy, it evokes a mood of quiet melancholy. The island of Brynos, where the action takes place, is a land of natural beauty and the happiest, but "one of the least famous islands" of Greece. The scene is quiet as the story opens: "The earth sighed as it turned on its course; the shadow of night crept gradually along the Mediterranean, and Asia was left in darkness."

But there is an uneasiness, a tension, in the air behind the quiet. "A confused starlight, already apprehensive of the still unrisen moon, fell upon the tiers of small houses. . . ." This tone of quiet apprehension, maintained throughout the book, points to the arrival of the "precious burden"—the birth of Christ—that is soon to come. The tone shows itself in the characters, too, who live in quiet desperation. Chrysis, who is happy temporarily because of her love for Pamphilus (a love destroyed, incidentally, by circumstance—a chance meeting of her sister and Pamphilus which results in their falling in love), says: "I am happy because I love Pamphilus—Pamphilus the anxious, Pamphilus the stupid. Why cannot someone tell him that it is not necessary to suffer so about living." But she herself suffers as Pamphilus does: "And a low exasperated sigh escaped her, the protest we make at the preposterous, the incorrigible beloved."

Character portrayal develops out of this stylistic and structural tension. The conflict is inner; the characters are unable to achieve a harmonious balance between their own inner compulsions towards beauty, virtue, wisdom, and love and the world they live in. Style and structure join to convey their turmoil and calm, their despair and hopes, the calm of their meditation, and the emotional intensity of their highly developed sensibilities. It is these qualities in Pamphilus and Chrysis that give them what Simo calls "the secret of living." Observing the priest of Aesculapius and Apollo, who is like them, Simo says: "People like that have some secret about living. Why don't they tell it to us outright, instead of wrapping it up in a mystery and ceremonial? They know something that prevents their blundering about, as we do. Yes, what am I doing here . . . but playing the fool? Blundering, advising in things I know nothing about . . . Pamphilus has some of that secret too. And that woman from Andros had it, too . . . there is something of the priest trying to make its way in him." These people stand in contrast, as Simo's words show, to characters like Chremes and Sostrata, Pamphilus' mother, who are bound to themselves and to the kind of social convention that, for example, would compel Pamphilus to marry a girl he doesn't love. Simo recognizes their superiority in sensibility, in love, in compassion, and in their wisdom that comes from their higher sensibility; and his final acceptance of Glycerium into his home marks the beginning of his humanity.

The moral is clear enough. Exquisitely as *The Woman* is constructed—and it wouldn't do to underestimate its poetic qualities—the characters resemble philosophical concepts too much to be convincing as living, actual people. Most of the tension arises from internal monologues, and there is a good deal of philosophizing without corresponding embodiment in concrete, realistic action. *The Woman*, like the three-minute plays, stands as evidence of both the excellence and the inadequacy of the romantic and poetic side of Wilder's vision. Lacking a counterpart in realistic, objective presentation of external conflict, this side of his vision falls into sentimentalism and his characters take on the coloration of romantic *Weltschmerz*. The poetic tendencies of the style—effective as they are—and the intrinsically romantic nature of the materials tend to render the moral and religious themes remote from actual life and reduce their claim to serious consideration. In order to be convincing, themes such as Wilder's require the inclusion of some degree of direct, actual experience. Unleavened and untested by a presentation of their antithetical elements, they lapse into sentimentality and romantic mysticism and lack the inclusiveness a fully developed vision should have.

Looking back over this period of early works, Wilder told Ross

Parmenter: "For years I shrank from describing the modern world. I was alarmed at finding a way of casting into generalization the world of doorbells and telephones. And now [1938], though many of the subjects will often be of the past, I like to feel that I accept the twentieth century, not only as a fascinating age to live in, but as assimilable stuff to think with."[9] He actually began to "accept" his own time soon after *The Woman* was published; for in November 1931, a year after it appeared, he brought out his first works dealing with contemporary America: *The Long Christmas Dinner and Other Plays in One Act.* His extreme swing away from aestheticism (that is, poetic treatment of intrinsically poetic materials derived from literary sources rather than life itself) to comic irony, contemporary American settings, and greater realism in these plays indicates his awareness that these latter elements were needed as correctives to the romantic sentimentalism, remoteness, and stylistic preciousness that had plagued his third novel.

Whether or not the Gold attack had anything to do with this change is hard to determine. It is possible that it—and the attacks a year earlier by the literary radicals upon his intellectual kinsmen, Irving Babbitt, Paul Elmer More, and Norman Foerster—convinced Wilder that it was time to bring his humanism out of the museum he had consigned it to in *The Woman* and into dynamic relationship with his own time. In any case, these plays reveal that he was probing at this time for a mythical structure and a technical method that would enable him not only to provide a faithful representation of the facts of American life but to reveal the spirit of religious humanism which he felt was still alive in America.

CHAPTER 3

Toward an American Perspective

IN his interview with Walther Tritsch in 1931, Wilder declared that "the real Americanism that will be important in the future is belief in the significance and even in the concealed implications of every event. It is precisely the same thing as the much abused doctrines of predestination and inward asceticism. In daily life this belief sometimes takes well-known, grotesque forms, such as when the money one has earned is looked upon as proof of God's mercy or justice. But that is only the ridiculous side of a very deep and fruitful life feeling. Just think of what it means to every American to believe himself permanently, directly, and responsibly bound to world destiny. The significance that this belief imparts to the simplest dealings and simplest events seems to me the beginning of all achievement. Such a trend precedes all great cultures."[1] Wilder's extensive study of the theatre in Europe during this period, along with his growing conviction that America and modern life could provide him with suitable literary material, brought him the technical and philosophical foundations he needed to bring his themes to the present and his drama out of books and onto the stage.

I The Long Christmas Dinner

The plays in *The Long Christmas Dinner* (1931) represent his first successful work for the theatre. The narrative elements that made most of the three-minute plays difficult if not impossible to stage are either not present in this volume or are incorporated into the action by use of a chorus-narrator. Set in the present and involving for the most part American characters of unpretentious origin, these plays comprise Wilder's closest approach to realism in the theatre, his first attempt at a colloquial style, his closest approach to conventional plotting, and his first successful attempt at the dramatic fusion of nonrealistic and realistic materials.

"Love and How to Cure it," "Queens of France," and "Such Things Only Happen in Books" all have well-made plots or slice-of-life presentation; and "The Long Christmas Dinner," "Pullman Car Hiawatha," and "The Happy Journey to Trenton and Camden" reveal theatricalist elements later perfected in *Our Town* and *The Skin of Our Teeth*. The first three of these plays are realistic in the sense that the presentation is objective, prosaic, and slice-of-life as opposed to the subjective, religious, poetic presentations of *The Angel That Troubled the Waters*. The themes are still moral, subjective, and aesthetic in the manner of the three-minute plays; but they arise from actions presented objectively enough to be enacted.

Moreover, the characters of these one-act plays develop with enough individuality to be identifiable as specific persons rather than two-dimensional embodiments of abstractions; and they gain complexity through irony. The central character of "Queens of France," for example, is a swindling New Orleans lawyer named Cahusac who defrauds simple, romantic-minded and spiritually impoverished women by telling them they are the lost successors to the French crown. The action takes place in a specific place (New Orleans) at a specific time (1869). Like the lawyer, the three women who come and go during the action are individualized as well as typed. Gullible and spiritually starved, each becomes more hilariously arrogant and imperious as she grows more convinced that she is indeed the Queen of France; and of course the more convinced each one becomes, the easier it is for Cahusac, as "representative of the Historical Society in Paris," to get her contributions towards the Restoration. As an individual, each makes her own peculiar response to her "rise" in station,. But while the women are ridiculous, they are also pathetic because of the emptiness which makes them susceptible to Cahusac's fantastic story. Comic irony turns to pathos near the end of the play when Cahusac discards the schoolteacher, Mlle. Pointevin, who has run out of money. She says: "It is all very strange. You know, M'su Cahusac, I think there may have been a mistake somewhere. It was so beautiful while it lasted. It made even schoolteaching a pleasure . . ."

More didactic but likewise ironic is "Love and How to Cure It," a realistic fable about love. As in "Queens of France," its theme arises from a concrete action involving specific, individualized characters. A medical student named Arthur has threatened to kill a shallow Cockney girl, Linda, who has spurned his love. The plot consists of the efforts by Linda, her Aunt Rowena, and Joey—all theatre people—to dissuade him. Arthur enters with a revolver hidden beneath his opera cape; and, during the action, Joey, a comedian, convinces Arthur that people who shoot the persons they love really love themselves and want to be noticed rather than loved in return. Arthur learns his lesson and leaves. But while he is repulsive to Linda because he is so "hot and excited and breathing so hard," it is Linda—"impersonal, remote, almost sullen"—who, in her cruel repudiation of the passionate Arthur, is the more culpable party and represents the same reprehensible coldness to love that characterized Dona Clara in *The Bridge* and Blair in *The Cabala*.

While these two plays show Wilder bringing some of the irony of his first two novels to the stage, "Such Things Only Happen in Books" reveals his increasing awareness that his works would henceforth have to deal more directly with life as he observed it. This play is a satire about a writer who, oblivious to the teeming life about him, complains that he has no plots for his stories. He has too much "literary conscience" to use such banal plots as "the plot that murderers always steal back to the scene of their crime and gloat over the place," or the plot that "all married women of thirty-five have lovers." Such things, he maintains, only happen in books. "Books and plays," he says, "are a quiet, harmless fraud about life." Believing that life really has no such interesting plots, he is totally unaware of what goes on about him: His wife is having an affair with the young doctor who is treating their maid; the maid has been burned accidentally by her escaped-convict brother whom she has been hiding in the novelist's house; and a man who murdered his father several years before returns to get the money hidden in the novelist's house, but his sister has already been there and taken the money with the unwitting help of the novelist.

The "well-made," complicated plot of this play is used only once again—in *The Matchmaker*, where Wilder parodies this type of plotting. While he retained the lesson the play taught about the artist's looking to life for his materials, he wanted a greater realism than such artificial plotting could give. He wanted to portray both the specific action and the universal idea imbedded in it, and contrived plotting of external events did not serve this purpose. The other three plays in the volume reflect his attempt to bring together the concreteness of incident and character that mark the above-mentioned plays with non-realistic technical devices. "The Long

Christmas Dinner," "Pullman Car Hiawatha," and "The Happy Journey to Trenton and Camden" are works in which he tries for the first time to affirm the presence of universal religious and moral values in the everyday lives of Americans.

His theories of drama were worked out in the making of these plays, and they are ones that accommodate a vision in which the microcosm of ordinary American life is related to what he called "the All, the Everywhere, and the Always." His interest in the expressionism of Strindberg and Elmer Rice shows that he was aware of the Scylla and Charybdis of too much and too little realism in the drama and wanted to avoid both. After seeing a production of one of Strindberg's works, for instance, he maintained that its failure was due to an excess of realism. On another occasion he observed that Rice's *Life Is Real* was too much of a thesis play; the ideas overwhelmed the action and reduced it to mere illustration. What he wanted was both the technical freedom that expressionism could offer and the faithful presentation of life and conventional restraints of concrete realism—"reality," as he wrote later,[2] rather than verisimilitude.

The dramaturgy Wilder developed in these three plays is what John Gassner has called "theatricalism."[3] Its outstanding feature is its frank admission that the action on stage is a play and not the representation of actual life that realism purports to achieve. Wilder stated, in the introduction he wrote for *Three Plays,* that he became dissatisfied with the theatre in the 1920s because he was "unable to lend credence" to what he regarded as the "childish attempts" of the realistic theatre "to be real." The drama, he said, is "based upon a pretense and its very nature calls out a multiplication of pretenses." What he objected to specifically in realistic stagecraft was the presence of properties and settings which he felt detracted from the frankly make-believe nature of stage drama. All that was needed for a good play was a "platform and a passion or two." "Have you ever noticed," he asked, "that in the plays of Shakespeare no one—except occasionally a ruler—ever sits down? There were not even chairs on the English or Spanish stages in the time of Elizabeth I."[4] More positively, he believed that the theatre should be like a festival—in the tradition of the Classical Greek theatre—with the audience playing a role either as participants or as vitally involved observers for whom life is being interpreted.

"The Long Christmas Dinner," "Pullman Car Hiawatha," and "The Happy Journey" adumbrate the theatricalism that came into full flower in *Our Town* and *The Skin of Our Teeth*. The circular form of "Dinner" and the stage manager device and the bare or nearly bare stage of the other two plays are deliberate affronts to "fourth wall" realistic attempts to approximate actuality. In these three plays his purpose is to "make the opaque matters of everyday transparent, with a view . . . to discovering something."[5] Each of the plays is based upon everyday matters—often the most trivial ones—in which "something" is discovered. Events in the lives of the characters are presented objectively, for the most part, but are related to a larger cosmological and metaphysical frame-work by unrealistic stage techniques. In "Pullman Car Hiawatha" and "The Happy Journey" a Stage Manager—a latter-day chorus—sets the stage or interprets the action, while in "The Long Christmas Dinner" a cyclical or circular form suggests a relationship between the recurring events on stage and "destiny."

The theme that the smallest events of ordinary life have a significance beyond what they seem to have thus arises out of the conflict between the realistic and nonrealistic modes of presentation. In order to get beyond the surface "appearance" of meaningless trivia, Wilder demolishes its claim to reality on the factual, concrete level, and puts the action on a moral, philosophical, or theological level. Hence, in "The Happy Journey" the characters, a humble American family, take a trip in an automobile that consists of four chairs set upon a low platform on a stage which has no scenery. The characters are engaged from the beginning in ordinary, "unimportant" activities. At the opening the boy Arthur is playing marbles, the girl Caroline talking to some friends, Ma Kirby putting on her hat. The dialogue is not heightened in any way. It is the everyday speech of unsophisticated, simple people:

> Ma: Where's your pa? Why isn't he here? I declare we'll never get started.
> Arthur: Ma, where's my hat? I guess I don't go if I can't find my hat.

The journey to Camden includes such common events as stopping at a gas station, eating hot dogs, and reading billboards, and has as its purpose a visit with the daughter Beulah. But the verisimilitude of slice-of-life is absent because it is destroyed as the play is enacted—by presence of the Stage Manager, by pantomine of the actors, and by absence of scenery and real properties.

Thematic and dramatic purposes come together by this method

as the "Act in Eternity." The audience is constantly reminded that
what they are seeing is theatre, not actual life, that life is being interpreted, not shown as actuality. The journey to Camden is a happy one, paradoxically, because these unimportant events are important, being by implication significant events in a meaningful
cosmological process. Ma Kirby, the central character, attaches a
moral-religious meaning to each incident, which either raises her
children to heights of joy or throws them into depths of depression.
The comic-ironic tone with which she is portrayed restrains the
potential seriousness of her moralizing and religious sentimentalism. Her moralizing and sentimentalism are, in fact, lightly
satirized—because they are conscious. The real meaning of her life
is seen when she is not self-consciously moral in what she does—in
her ecstasy, for instance, at Arthur's remorse for having offended
her; and in her singing, at the end, the song

> There were ninety and nine that safely lay
> In the shelter of the fold,
> But one was out on the hills away
> Far off from the gates of gold.

She is consciously moral—like Mrs. Antrobus, later, in *The Skin
of Our Teeth*—and consciously religious in her attitude and reac-
tions to actual, concrete incidents and things; but she is unconsciously moral in relation to her *real* purposes. The truth of her
life lies in what she is not entirely aware of (she sings the song
"absent-mindedly")—but which the audience sees. Ma Kirby's simple faith sustains her, gives her courage, and keeps her family going. She tells her daughter, whose baby has died at birth: "God
thought best, dear. God thought best. We don't understand why.
We just go on, honey, doin' our business." The theatricalism here,
breaking through external appearances, supports the idea that Ma
Kirby's real virtues lie beyond her superficially moralistic exterior.

"Pullman Car Hiawatha," the most ambitious and intricately
constructed of all these plays, has a symphonic structure which conveys the theme of universal harmony. The Stage Manager is used
here as the arranger and interpreter of the action, manipulating the
characters and scenes according to the idea he wants to illustrate. As
in "The Happy Journey" he plays various parts besides his own,
without any attempt at realism or individuality. After marking off
the outlines of the train on the stage floor, he calls the actors in,

director-like, and they enter carrying chairs to their "berths" or "compartments"—their respective marked-off places. The illusion of verisimilitude is, therefore, destroyed before the play begins, just as it is in "The Happy Journey."

But while in this play the family is individualized to some extent, the characters in "Pullman Car Hiawatha" are frankly types: "a maiden lady," "a middle-aged doctor," "an engineer going to California," an insane woman, a young couple, Harriet and Phillip. For, since the play is an allegory, the characters are types who fit into a scheme of ideas. Beginning with the dialogue of these de-individualized types (they are called by their positions on the train—"Compartment Two," "Lower Three"), the play proceeds from the chaotic life in the berths to the sound of the characters thinking—above which their individual thoughts are heard as soliloquies. The characters in the berths are busy with the trivia of life, as seen from the outside, but with more important, personal matters within their minds. In the opening movement the Stage Manager, directing the action like an orchestra conductor, calls for the scene to shift to the compartments and their occupants, Philip, Harriet, and the Insane Woman. The last two characters are suffering physically and mentally, respectively. At Harriet's death, the Stage Manager steps in again to direct the car's position "geographically, meteorologically, astronomically, theologically considered."

At this point, a second movement begins in which there is an ascending scale of sounds and rhythms, from the insects in the fields the train passes through to the music of the spheres, all of which join in a universal harmony. Personified are a town (Grover's Corners, Ohio), a field with all its animal and insect life, and the ghost of a workman killed while working on a bridge. Together with a tramp who sings a line from "The Road to Mandalay" by "Frank W. Service," these personifications represent the rhythms and sounds of life measured in minutes—of life as flux without apparent order. The Stage Manager says: "The minutes are gossips; the hours are philosophers; the years are theologians. The hours are philosophers with the exception of Twelve O'clock, who is also a theologian."

The hours, "beautiful girls dressed like Elihu Vedder's Pleiades," carry Roman numerals onto the stage and speak lines from Plato (Ten O'clock), Epictetus (Eleven O'clock) and St. Augustine (Twelve O'clock). Then the planets arrive, each with its individual

sound made by the actor playing the part, and the sounds of the
earth (all the characters in the play) join with those of the planets.

The third movement begins when the Insane Woman breaks in
on the earth's "sound" with the words, "Use me. Give me
something to do." She is led back to her guardian, whereupon the
Stage Manager announces the entrance of the archangels and the
"theological position of Pullman Car Hiawatha." The music motif
continues and the sounds of the characters and planets resume to
serve as the background for the dead Harriet's recitation of a
prayer—and all make up the sound of the solar system. In each of
the three movements the rhythms of life blend into harmonious
relation with a larger whole—first the earth, then the universe, and
finally the solar system. The most humble of the human characters,
the tramp, directs the latter part of the second and third movements
"like the conductor of an orchestra," the function the Stage
Manager fulfills in the first movement and most of the second.

Counterpointing the harmony in each movement are the two sufferers, Harriet and the Insane Woman. Harriet, like Emily Webb in
Our Town, comes to realize the blindness of humans to the gift of
life; and, having been unaware of it and ungrateful for it herself,
she protests to the Archangels Michael and Gabriel that she is unfit
to go with them—she wants to be punished. The Insane Woman,
whose insanity reveals itself in her dialogue with the attendant and
the nurse in the first movement, displays insights sane persons lack
in her dialogue with the two archangels. In their thematic dis-
sonance, these two characters serve the double functions of
emphasizing the ignorance of human beings of their "position" as
part of a harmonious, meaningful whole (life, like Pullman Car
Hiawatha, has a destination) and of illustrating the Old Testament
(Job) and Greek (particularly Aeschylus) concepts of purpose in suffering. That they are in compartments rather than berths, as the
other characters are, signifies, perhaps, their special nature as persons having the wisdom of those schooled by affliction.

This remarkably constructed allegory, combining all levels of
time and space and relating the life of the mind to the life of the
universe, is of all the early plays the closest to *Our Town* and *The
Skin of Our Teeth* technically and thematically. In the later, full-
length plays, however, Wilder utilizes the concreteness of the individual family found in "The Long Christmas Dinner" and "The
Happy Journey" to achieve a more realistic microcosm than he
achieved in this play. But while lack of an adequate dramatic focus

deprives "Pullman Car Hiawatha" of sufficient dramatic tension, its movement is, after all, musical, blending discordant or dissonant elements into harmonies that dissolve rather than intensify conflict. Dramatically considered, Wilder's vision in this play of an harmonious universe in which all contradictions are ultimately resolved has the weakness that critics like Cleanth Brooks and Allen Tate found in "Platonic" poetry, whose propaganda, they felt, is exclusive, untested by struggle, and oversimplified; one admires its theatrical novelty but is unpersuaded by its propositions. Nevertheless, it might well have been made into a very good opera. "The Long Christmas Dinner," revised slightly by Wilder and set to music by the great German composer Paul Hindemith, was successful as an opera in both Europe and the United States in the early 1960s; and given the even more palpable musical structure of "Pullman Car Hiawatha," its possibilities for success as an opera would seem very good.

Wilder did not follow up these first dramatic ventures into the contemporary American scene until 1938 when *Our Town* appeared. In the meantime he translated and adapted a play that was thoroughly anti-realistic—Obey's *Lucréce*, for Katharine Cornell in 1932—and wrote his most realistic novel, *Heaven's My Destination* (1935). The mythical structure that would permit him to combine a convincingly objective view of American life with a non-realistic portrayal of its relation with human destiny was still to be formulated. But if by 1935 he had not yet found the vehicle to carry his conviction that the great universal humanistic values could be found in American life, he was able to diagnose the moral illness of mid-depression America in humanistic terms in one of the best but least appreciated novels written in that era of proletarian and humanitarian panaceas, *Heaven's My Destination*.

II   Heaven's My Destination

What *The Woman of Andros* had lacked more than anything else was an effective and concrete antagonist to its main characters to give dramatic tension and expression to their inner conflicts. The spiritually torpid society that failed to understand and appreciate Chrysis and Pamphilus was inadequately developed, with the result that the humane concepts they embodied were not clearly defined in action and their longings for religious certitude and for a greater human consciousness in love appeared maudlin. Wilder corrected this weakness in *Heaven's My Destination* (1935) by shifting to the American scene and drawing it fully and realistically.

The chief character, George Brush, is a kind of Elmer Gantry in reverse; and it is possible that Wilder intended the book to be in part an answer to Sinclair Lewis. Like Gantry, Brush gets his early religious training in a Baptist college in the Middle West, has an early sexual experience with a girl from a small town, and runs into difficulty with believers and nonbelievers alike. But unlike Gantry he is a sincere believer himself; and, where Gantry profits from his hypocrisy, Brush suffers for his true belief. The sarcasm Brush encounters as a believer is reminiscent at times of the tone Lewis used toward Gantry and his fellow clergymen. But while Gantry lives in an America of false belief and hypocritical clergymen, Brush lives in a nation that has lost its spiritual heritage and sense of purpose, and Wilder treats him with a good deal more compassion than Lewis accords Gantry. As a result, Brush is a more complex creation.

Heaven's My Destination is, among other things, a testimonial to the effectiveness of a well-managed narrative perspective, which permits Wilder better than in any of his previous fiction to express his themes through action rather than assertion. The narrative is so objective, in fact, that Wilder was chastised for failing to state unequivocally his attitude toward Brush. He told Ross Parmenter in 1938, "My last novel was written as objectively as it could be done and the result has been that people tell me that it has meant to them things as diverse as a Pilgrim's Progress of the religious life and an extreme sneering at sacred things, a portrait of a saint on the one hand and a ridiculous fool jeered at by the author on the other."[6] Such misinterpretations were a result, surely, of the failure by those readers to detect Wilder's marvelous comic irony, which functions best when the author keeps himself and his comments out of the story, as he does here. The objective presentation is itself ironic. Brush is both a fool and a saint, but that fact has to be inferred from the dialectical development of the action. Despite the general failure of the reading public and the critics to understand the book, Wilder rightly defended his narrative strategy when he told Parmenter that "the ultimate point of view . . . the beholder should take upon the action [in a literary work] is nowhere indicated, but is distributed throughout the work by a series of strains and stresses in selection and emphasis."

Midwestern Baptist, moral reformer, and book salesman, Brush represents an amalgamation in their most innocuous and comical forms of the fundamentalist, the humanitarian, and that archetype of the materialistic society, the salesman. He symbolizes what one critic called "America in its awkward age"[7]—an America attempting naively to reconcile its disparate spiritual and materialistic qualities. Brush's innocence is the naiveté not only of the fundamentalist who rejects the theory of evolution and insists upon a literal interpretation of the Bible but also of the humanitarian who, ignorant of evil, is betrayed by both his own lower impulses and those of others to commit acts he regards as sinful. The action—set in the Midwestern Bible Belt, stronghold of evangelism—takes place during the depression of the 1930s when panaceas for reform were perhaps more prevalent than at any other period in American history and when the nation was suffering most from the materialistic binge of the 1920s. The clash that results when the ingenuous but spiritually healthy Brush brings his religious and moral principles to bear upon a society sick with skepticism and moral apathy is at once comical and pitiful.

Out of that conflict arise the implied themes of a faith purified of ignorance, of moral principles based upon both tolerance of human frailties and understanding of evil, and of skepticism tempered by moral concern. Brush symbolizes both the best and the worst in the American religious and moral tradition. He can sell books even during a depression; but the religion he tries to peddle has almost no market. During the year covered by the novel, he makes a sales tour of the Middle West and Southwest and meets a cross-section of society which rejects his preaching and moralizing. His futility is a compound of absurdity and well-meaning goodness. His religion has come to him by way of conversion during his sophomore year in college by a sixteen-year-old girl who, he learns later, was a drug addict. His courses at college have included "How to approach strangers on the subject of salvation" and "Arguments in Sacred Debate." Thus armed with both evangelical fervor and the know-how of salesmanship, he accosts people he meets with "Brother, can I talk to you about the most important thing in life?" At one point his belief in *ahimsa* (influence of Gandhi) leads him to try to help a hold-up man avoid arrest, which Brush regards as a form of cruelty. His attempt fails; and, when Brush is brought to trial, the judge, who is one of the few characters in the book who are aware of the virtue as well as the naiveté of Brush's theories of *ahimsa* and voluntary poverty, tells Brush without irony: "Well, it's all sort of poetical and sentimental, Mr. Brush; but it's very unlike the facts of life.

And it seems to be based upon a profound misunderstanding of the criminal's mind."

Far as Brush's religious and humanitarian principles are from the "facts of life," they are humane; he exasperates people almost beyond endurance, but he also helps some of them, even after they have mistreated him. He promises to take responsibility for the child of a dying man who has almost cruelly abused him, for instance, and saves another from self-destruction at the risk of his own life.

Society, Wilder makes it clear, needs Brush and his values, whatever their weaknesses. The people Brush meets are typically sophisticated and cynical on the surface but resigned to despair beneath it; and they can find no way out of their perdition. Among the people he encounters are a man named Roberts at Camp Morgan, who has nightmares and is nearly mad with worry; three roomers at a Kansas City boarding house who despise Brush because he is a constant reminder of their own spiritual emptiness; a disillusioned intellectual, Burkin, who scorns Brush's religious naiveté. Invariably they become angry with Brush and abuse him but fail to change him to their ways, which they try to do as much as Brush tries to change them.

Brush is all heart. That his otherwise admirable principles lack intelligence is suggested by his conflicts with intelligent people in the incidents involving Jessie Mayhew and Burkin. In the first of these incidents Brush becomes fond of the bright young college girl until he learns that she "believes in" evolution: "Brush almost whispered: 'You don't think the Bible'd tell a lie, do you? Do you mean you can't see there's a difference as big as the whole world between a human being with a soul and a monkey jumping around in a tree?' There was an awful silence. Then Brush put another fateful question: 'You don't believe in women smoking cigarettes, do you?' " The girl refuses to discuss these absurdities with Brush and dismisses him from her mind—though not without difficulty.

But the intellectual Burkin does discuss them with him. An unemployed motion-picture director who has been mistakenly jailed as a peeping-tom, Burkin, brilliant and cynical, is the opposite of Brush. He is contemptuous of the Bible, the middle class, and Brush. After Brush has related his religious and evangelical experiences, Burkin says: "You live in a foggy, unreal, narcotic dream . . . Listen, benny, can't you see that what you call religion is just the shiverings of the cowardly? It's just what people tell themselves because they haven't got the guts to look the facts of life and death in the face. If you'd gone to a respectable college you'd have had the chance to get wise to these things. You've probably never been exposed once in your whole life to anybody who really had any practice in thinking."

Burkin's skepticism is a necessary corrective to the extremes of Brush's faith. One is reminded here of Emerson's observation that in the essays of Montaigne the cause of belief is served by a healthy skepticism; and of Arnold's argument for a balance between "sweetness" and "light." Burkin's intelligence, inadequate as it is by itself, is the indispensable counterpart ot Brush's faith. In his attack, Burkin strikes at the most vulnerable points in Brush's religion: "Burkin plunged into primitive man and the jungle; he came down through the nature myths; he hung the earth in astronomical time. He then exposed the pretensions of subjective religious experience; the absurdity of conflicting prayers, man's egotistic terror before extinction."

Yet, like most of the others Brush meets in his travels, Burkin is a sick spirit; his sickness—cynicism—is manifested by a "nervous twitch" he cannot hide. And in the conflict between his heartless rationalism and Brush's mindless fundamentalism, the higher synthesis is enlightened faith. Brush's immediate reaction to Burkin's attack is: "When you began I thought you were going to say things that would stick in your mind and trouble me"; but then he adds: "you don't know anything about religion until you start to live it. All you've done is *think* about it as though it were . . . as though it were a *fish* a long ways off." So they separate unreconciled, thought and feeling, reason and intuition, intellect and morality, each needing the other; they are unresolved antitheses whose fusion is unlikely to occur until Brush's fundamentalist faith and humanitarian morals establish themselves on a sound humanistic foundation. In his present state of awkwardness Brush is unequipped to deal effectively with his opposition. His inability to distinguish the real sources of evil, for example, leads him to spend his time and energy combatting such minor sins as smoking by women; at the same time he is being gulled by acquaintances who have taken him to a house of prostitution. During his brief loss of faith following the breakup of his short-lived marriage, he observes bitterly that: "I've broken all the Ten Commandments, except two. I never killed anybody and I never made any graven images. . . ."

Wilder thus directs his double-edged satire toward the kind of

Elmer Gantry cynicism seen in Burkin and Brush's fellow boarders in Kansas City on the one hand and Brush's naiveté on the other; he attacks by implication both the doctrines of social amelioration and human perfectibility so dear to humanitarian reformers (including Marxists like Gold) and the spiritual sterility of rationalism. Noticeably absent from this proletarian-age novel is any suggestion of class conflict or of the presence of economic or natural forces that overwhelmed the "common man," for instance, in Steinbeck's *In Dubious Battle* and *The Grapes of Wrath*, where the human plight is portrayed in terms of the misuse of nature, both physical and human. Nature rebels against the overcultivation of the Oklahoma topsoil in *The Grapes of Wrath;* and this depletion and the predatory economic system drive the hapless farmers from the land they love. Steinbeck's implied solution to the problem is social: political and economic reforms are needed to restore the balance between man and nature, between a bountiful nature and the men who are instinctively a part of it but are forced, because of economic circumstances, to misuse it.

Wilder's diagnosis of the human condition, on the contrary, is moral, inner. When Brush comes into conflict with a bank manager by refusing to collect interest on his savings, he attacks the fear that makes banks necessary: "No one who has saved up in a bank can really be happy." The power of banks would not exist if the fear they feed on were abolished. Although such a view does not solve the problems of the dust-bowl farmer or the factory worker who is at the mercy of economic cycles, it attacks indirectly the immorality of a social system that preys upon human frailties. Fear, greed, cynicism toward human motives are the real "forces" that need to be combated.

Such strengthening of the will, Wilder intimates, is up to the individual. Social and political reforms cannot—should not—do the job. With Thoreau, Wilder prescribes a stronger moral fiber as the only true antidote to poverty and social injustice. Though Brush represents "goodness" in its "awkward age" (Wilder chose as his epigraph for the book a passage from *The Woman of Andros:* "Of all the forms of genius, goodness has the longest awkward age"), his generosity, his devotion to the spiritual and material welfare of others, and his desire to conduct his life by a moral code rather than by acceptance of the world as he finds it, comprise essential elements in the improvement of the human condition.

Brush's growth toward maturity is slow, but his obsession with self-improvement offers hope that his goodness will eventually be balanced by intelligence. He learns in the course of his travels, for example, that belief in evolution may not be immoral. At the end of the book he goes through a "crisis" that leads him into temporary disbelief; but after his faith is renewed by an expression of confidence in him by another man of faith—a dying Catholic priest whom Brush never meets—he continues with the same activities he pursued at the beginning, except that now he meets a waitress who is reading Darwin and arranges to put her through college. Purged of some of their worst elements of ignorance and narrowness, his faith and morals are more secure as the story ends; and he is considerably more prepared for the "business of living" than before. The great gulf between the humanistic ideal as Wilder conceives it and the "real" facts of American life is not bridged here, and Wilder gives no indication that it will be; but he leaves no doubt that it can be. If it is to be done, faith based upon humanistic ethics is requisite.

George Brush inevitably reminds one of that nineteenth-century peddler of hard-goods and good deeds, Amos Bronson Alcott, and *Heaven's My Destination* belongs to the tradition of *Candide, Tom Jones,* and *Huckleberry Finn* in its episodic depiction of an innocent journeying through various facets of society. Wilder undoubtedly had great fun elaborating the traveling salesman - farmer's daughter tale into a full-length work, but his picture of the ailments of contemporary society is as grim as it is comical. And because it does not limit itself to such specific problems of the 1930s as Pittsburgh and the breadlines, it escapes both the topicality and the oversimplification that have sent many of its contemporaries in fiction into oblivion.

CHAPTER 4

Three Theatricalist Plays

IN the fall of 1930 Wilder accepted an invitation from his ex-classmate at Oberlin and Yale, Robert Hutchins, to teach at the University of Chicago, where he lectured for half a year during each of the next six years. In 1935, he met Gertrude Stein, who was also giving lectures at the University; he became her lifelong friend, confidant, and champion. They had long conversations which Wilder later summarized in part in introductions to her *Four in America, Geographical History of America,* and *Narration: Four Lectures.* She taught him, he recounted later, to ignore the critics and to write "as though no one else were listening"[1]—useful advice for a sensitive person like Wilder who had already suffered from virulent critical attacks and was to undergo more in the next decade. More important, she enabled him to bring his aesthetic theories and humanism into cohesion and to apply them affirmatively to contemporary American society.

I *Gertrude Stein and Wilder's Literary Theories*

Everything, including the statement of Professor Wager at Oberlin that every great work was written this morning, "fell into place as he listened to her," wrote a *Time* reporter after an interview with Wilder.[2] She confirmed his humanistic conviction that the eternal human truths were to be found in literary masterpieces, and she then put forth the corollary that those truths can also be observed in American life. She made a distinction—which corresponded roughly to the dualistic one of humanism between body and mind—between human nature and human mind. Human nature, she said, clings to "self," to identity, to location in time and place, and to survival; but human mind, in Wilder's words, "knowing no time and identity, can realize [a nonself situation] as an objective fact of experience."[3] Human mind contemplates pure existing and pure creating, she maintained, and can be observed in masterpieces which record the timeless and universal; but it can also be seen in the America which has always identified itself with world destiny.

While Wilder portrayed the mystical identification of the American with human destiny in its naive form in *Heaven's My Destination*, it was in *Our Town* and in *The Skin of Our Teeth* that he set it forth in conjunction with his fully developed theory which, because of its nature, found the stage a more suitable medium than the novel. This theory and the part Gertude Stein played in helping Wilder formulate it can be seen in his introductions to her three books on America and in his "Thoughts on Playwrighting," which he wrote in 1941 for Augusto Centeno's *The Intent of the Artist*.[4]

Recalling his conversations with Gertrude Stein, Wilder said in his introduction to *Four in America* that her distinction between human nature and human mind first arose when they discussed the qualities peculiar and common to great writers. Great writers, he said, glossing Stein, possessed a "certain relation to the problems of identity and time." The masterpiece gets its materials from human nature but is of the human mind; and contemplation of the literary masterpiece effects "pure existing" in the sense that the human mind emerges and perceives the eternal and universal in the individual. This human mind that emerges from masterpieces and reveals the truth latent in the minds of all men also appears under certain geographical conditions, she maintained. Wilder wrote: "Miss Stein, believing in the intermittent emergence of the Human Mind and its record in literary masterpieces to be the most important manifestation of human culture, observed that these emergences were dependent upon the geographical situations in which the author lived. The valley-born and the hill-bounded tended to exhibit a localization in their thinking and an insistence on identity with all the resultant traits that dwell in Human Nature; flat lands or countries surrounded by long straight lines of the sea were conducive to developing the power of abstraction."[5]

Gertrude Stein maintained that the American, in his detachment from time and place, is the best living source of evidence of the eternal existing in the individual. In the United States the human mind is "distributed throughout the people," where the writer may observe it in the daily life of ordinary people. Thus while the realistic writer, by implication, tends to confine himself to the literal recording of human nature, the less insular and more imaginative writer—the producer of masterpieces—uses human nature as his materials but goes beyond its surface appearance to the realm of human mind or of eternal ideas.

His acceptance of Gertrude Stein's essentially Platonic view of twentieth-century America—and the relative failure of *Heaven's My Destination* to gain critical and popular favor—convinced Wilder that drama is superior to fiction as an art form because the theatre audience sees "pure existing," while the reader of fiction is asked to accept what the author says arbitrarily *about* the life he presents. In "Thoughts on Playwrighting," he listed "four fundamental conditions of the drama" that distinguish it from the other arts. In combination with the theories of America derived from Gertrude Stein, they show the aesthetic bases of *Our Town* and *The Skin of Our Teeth*. The conditions are: that the theatre performance requires many collaborators; that it is "addressed to the group mind"; that it is "based upon a pretense and its very nature calls out a multiplication of pretenses"; and, finally, that the action "takes place in a perpetual present."

Of the first of these conditions he stated that, unlike the novel or painting, the drama is not the "product of one governing will"—of the artist or the author. Collaborators such as actors and directors, who are vital to drama, necessarily mean variation in interpretation of a play, which of course is a problem to the playwright. The disadvantage is compensated for, however, because "the theater presents certain vitalities of its own so inviting that the writer is willing to receive them in compensation for this inevitable variation from an exact image" and because "the dramatist through working in the theater learns not merely to take account of the presence of the collaborators, but to derive advantage from them; and he learns, above all, to organize the play in such a way that its strength lies not in appearances beyond his control, but in the succession of events and in the unfolding of an idea, in narration."

The audience witnesses the play as a succession of events illustrating a general idea, and through the "disposition of events" the author maintains a control over the idea "so complete that the distortions effected by the physical appearance of actors, by the fancies of scene painters and the misunderstandings of directors, fall into relative insignificance." Because of the "expectancy of the group mind," the problem of time, the absence of a narrator, and the "element of pretense," the drama "carries the art of narration to a higher power than the novel or epic poem." Confronted with the possibility of misinterpretation, the writer is forced to attend to the "laws of narration, its logic and its deep necessity of presenting a unifying idea stronger than its mere collection of happenings."

Wilder felt he could achieve in the drama what he had been trying to do in the novel without complete satisfaction to himself: eliminate the author from the narrative scene and allow the characters to reveal themselves by means of (1) "highly characteristic utterances, (2) concrete occasions in which character defines itself under action, and (3) a conscious preparation of the text whereby the actor may build upon the suggestions in the role according to his own abilities." The author provides some signs of individuality for the actor to go by, but he leaves much of the individual interpretation to the actor and concentrates his efforts upon the achievement of the general idea. The presentation is, therefore, more objective than in the novel because the "dogmatic assertions" of the omniscient novelist about his characters are eliminated. The result is that the stage can do a better job of combining the particular and the universal truth.

In elaborating the second condition of drama, Wilder maintained that because the theatre is addressed to the group mind, it is a kind of ritual or festival in which the audience is an indispensable part of the production. Without an audience a play would "fall to pieces and absurdity," for the excitement of pretending requires a throng. The audience is both spectator and participant; thus in *The Matchmaker* the characters—like the Stage Manager in *Our Town*, Lily Sabina in *The Skin of Our Teeth*, and the Watchman in *The Alcestiad*—address the audience directly. In theatricalist style the audience is reminded that it is seeing a play. But, he admitted, "a group mind presupposes if not a lowering of standards, a broadening of the fields of interest." Drama cannot assume, as the other arts can, a trained audience capable of understanding or being interested in special aspects of life, such as the historical or the psychological, that are not generally known. If the audience is to play its part in the "festival" that is the theatre, it has to have before it material it understands.

This last point was a source of irritation to critics—notably to Francis Fergusson[6]—who felt that Wilder, unlike T. S. Eliot, compromised his art by trying to please or make himself understandable to the mass mind. But Wilder did not share Eliot's contempt for the group mind; on the contrary, Wilder the democrat wanted to reach enlightened mass audiences in order to remind them of what was best in their cultural heritage. The question of whether or not his appeal to the group mind represents a lowering of standards in drama depends ultimately upon whether or not the material that makes such an appeal is successfully integrated in a vision that does not oversimplify or falsify the life it represents. Fergusson contended that there are two sets of materials in *Our Town* and in *The Skin of Our Teeth;* one set is directed toward the "greater number"; and the other, the philosophical, toward those of greater understanding. Fergusson also asserted that both plays suffer from this division; but the presence of two sets of materials is debatable—particularly in the case of *Our Town.* It is true, however, that both plays use subjects that consciously draw upon common experiences in the audience at all levels. The artistic effectiveness of this device is discussed in relation to these plays later in the chapter.

Wilder's third "condition"—that the theatre is a "world of pretense"—was his refutation in principle of "slice-of-life" realism. He contended that, since the theatre is a world of pretense straining toward a general truth, scenery and sets that tie the action to a specific time and place and are intended to effect a fourth-wall realism tend to deprive the audience of its imaginative participation and require it to accept as real what it knows is not. He cited the great drama of Greece and China and of Racine and Corneille as evidence that scenery and sets are not necessary to "reality," which Wilder distinguished from the verisimilitude of realism. In this, of course, he was supported by Aristotle, who placed scenery last in the hierarchy of parts of a play, and by the Chinese, whose classic drama had only placards to identify the scenery.

In explaining the fourth condition for drama, Wilder reiterated his belief that it is a higher type of narration than the novel. "A play visibly represents pure existing," he said. "A novel is what one mind, claiming to omniscience, asserts to have existed." The "pure existing" depicted by the drama made it for him the natural vehicle to express his mythical view of the "pure existing" American, which he had clarified during his association with Gertrude Stein. He felt that such a dramaturgy conjoined with such a mythical vision could restore the festive or ritual atmosphere that the theatre had always had in its greatest ages. At its best the stage play was a kind of religious ceremony in which the audience contemplated the ritual demonstration of the human condition and of the relationship of the individual to nature, to humanity, and to the cosmos.

In an introduction he wrote for the Heritage edition of *Oedipus*

Rex, he expressed regret that the great religious experience felt by Greek audiences is missing from the contemporary stage. The theatre, he said, "has lost one of its most powerful effects—the shudder and awe induced by the presence of the numinous, by the *tremendum* of religious experience. . . ." While Apollo was not in *Oedipus,* Wilder maintained that his presence was felt and that his will was the real subject of the play. The present age is not one in which a religious shudder and awe is likely to be felt as the Greek audiences felt it, but *Our Town* and *The Skin of Our Teeth* are attempts to recover for modern audiences the feeling that there is a meaningful relationship between the individual and nature, and mankind and the universe, and to restore to life those elements of mystery and love that are the basis for the affirmation of a higher presence.

II Our Town

Such a monumental ambition would be pretentious if handled in a grand manner and on the grand scale. But *Our Town* is pitched in a low key, has an almost pastoral setting, and involves the ordinary events in the lives of ordinary people; and *The Skin of Our Teeth* has strong elements of comedy and burlesque to counterbalance the potential pretentiousness of its themes. Both plays focus attention upon the life-ritual and are theatricalist, stylized dramas.

Wilder stated in the preface to *Three Plays* that "*Our Town* is not offered as a picture of life in a New Hampshire village; or as a speculation about conditions of life after death (that element I merely took from Dante's *Purgatory*). It is an attempt to find a value above all price for the smallest events of our daily life. I have made the claim as preposterous as possible, for I have set the village against the largest dimensions of time and place. The recurrent words in this play (few have noticed it) are 'hundreds,' 'thousands,' and 'millions.' Emily's joys and griefs, her algebra lessons and her birthday presents—what are they when we consider all the billions of girls who have lived, who are living, and who will live?"

The action—which takes place in Grover's Corners, New Hampshire, on specific days in the years between 1901 and 1913—portrays both the routine daily life and the major events in the lives of George Gibbs and Emily Webb and their families. Each act centers about a scene of the family life which is preceded by a street scene involving the casual conversation of such characters as the milkman, the constable, and the paper boy—town folk in general. Act I consists of scenes showing a complete day in the town and in the Webb and Gibbs households when George and Emily are growing up. In Acts II and III family scenes and the everyday street scenes are shown again but in relation, respectively, to the courtship and marriage of George and Emily and Emily's death.

But specific as the dates, places, and characters are—and Wilder provides all the important facts, including the history of the town, to individualize the action—it is immediately apparent that it is life rather than individual lives that is being enacted; that life is being presented rather than represented; and that the people, the place, and the time are the "All, the Everywhere and the Always." We are reminded, as we are in "The Happy Journey" and "Pullman Car Hiawatha," that this is a theatre play as the Stage Manager points to nonexistent properties which the audience is asked to imagine exist. And even as he is giving his detailed factual account of the town and its people, he violates the usual limitations of time sequence by using past, present, and future tenses concurrently; and Wilder achieves thereby on stage a present that encompasses all time—the action becomes an "Act in Eternity."

The Stage Manager presents the life on stage directly to the audience, addresses his comments about it to the audience, and at one point answers questions asked by actors planted in the audience. Like the property man in Chinese drama, he places the few properties on stage (which consist mainly of tables and chairs, ladders and planks); and, like the chorus in Greek theatre, he comments on the action, takes part in it himself, and functions as the author's mouthpiece. But in addition to his technical functions, he embodies the spirit of the town and selects and presents the scenes with a view to demonstrating the ideas behind them. For example, he announces in Act I that the play is to be a demonstration of how people grew up and married and lived and died "in the provinces north of New York at the beginning of the twentieth century," and he then offers scenes typical of the daily life in the Webb and Gibbs households. The metaphysical significance of the scenes is then expressed by George's sister Rebecca at the close of the act:

I never told you about that letter Jane Crofut got from her minister when she was sick. He wrote Jane a letter and on the envelope the address was like this: It said: Jane Crofut; the Crofut Farm; Grover's Corner; Sutton County; New Hampshire; United States of America.
  GEORGE: What's so funny about that?

REBECCA: But listen, it's not finished: the United States of America; Continent of North America; Western Hemisphere; the Earth; the Solar System; the Universe; the Mind of God——

This passage, prepared for by the previous presentation of actions specifically identifiable as to time and place but raised to the level of the eternal, anticipates the increasingly broadened scope of the action in acts II and III. Theatricalist technique by this means achieves a union of action and idea.

Our Town is a picture of the priceless value of even the most common and routine events in life and of the waste of life through failure to realize the value of every moment. Unaware of the value of life, the people of Grover's Corners live their lives banally and seldom get beneath or above the surface of life. Yet even what they do realize and experience is beyond price; and this is the paradox that pervades the play and is the source of its tension. The conflict is basically inner, between consciousness and unconsciousness or between awareness and appreciation of life and insensibility and self-preoccupation.

The artistic problem basic to *Our Town* is that of showing that the events of life are at once not all they could be because they are taken for granted—but are priceless. Wilder meets this problem by repeating the quotidian scenes and viewing them and the central actions of each act (growing up, love and marriage, and death) from different perspectives of time and space and different metaphysical vantage points. By relating the ordinary events in the lives of these ordinary people to a metaphysical framework that broadens with each act, he is able to portray life as being at once significant and trivial, noble and absurd, miraculous and humdrum.

The ordinary characterizes all the scenes and narrative passages, and this quality is reinforced by colloquial dialogue liberally sprinkled with platitudes. The "facts" the Stage Manager recites about Grover's Corners are unstartling, commonplace, and statistical; and the answers he gives to questions asked by the actors in the audience (a woman concerned about the drinking in the town, a man indignant about the lack of awareness of social injustice and inequality, and a lady wondering about the cultural level of the town) indicate that the townspeople give little thought to such things. In Act II the Stage Manager-Minister repeats the idea when he says the weddings he has performed are interesting "once in a thousand times," and in Act III even death itself is shown to be a very commonplace, unstartling, and unfrightening event. Repetition of the quotidian scene, however, transforms the ordinariness into ritual; and, when the dead Emily returns to observe and relive her twelfth birthday in Act III, she becomes aware that the daily life of the town and of the families was humdrum and commonplace because taken for granted and not fully appreciated.

The success of *Our Town* rests in no small degree on Wilder's ability to make the ordinary interesting and portray its intrinsic value without falling into bathos. Lacking the suspense that goes with a carefully plotted conflict between characters, the play admittedly draws heavily upon theatricalist novelty for fresh treatment of its materials; and much of its effect is owing to its appeal to audience nostalgia. But the material and the technical devices conceived for the benefit of the "group mind" have within them the seeds of a larger meaning; and this promise of a larger meaning gives suspense to the action. The people of Grover's Corners, being of the type Gertrude Stein called the "valley-born and the hill-bounded," exhibit the "localization in their thinking" that distinguishes them from their brethren living in flat country or on coastlines. Most of them never get very far from Grover's Corners during their lives; and most, like George and Emily, never care to. Their lack of interest in such abstractions as temperance, social equality, culture and beauty is characteristic of their kind, and the significance of their lives lies concealed in their pattern of living in the trivia of "human nature" that they are steeped in. Thus they do not try to find a concept in living as do Brush and Antrobus of *The Skin of Our Teeth*. Yet, the play says by implication that there is meaning even in lives in which there is no conscious and deeply felt guiding principle.

Each act has scenes (those involving such characters as the milkman, the constable, the paper boy) showing a simple bond of friendship among men and the routine family and community life. In Act I these scenes comprise the core of the action and represent the eternal rhythms of life; but in Acts II and III they become objective correlatives for humanistic and theological perspectives. In Act II, the love and marriage of George and Emily symbolize the universal rite uniting nature's physical and spiritual forces; and, in Act III, Emily's death and brief return to life represent the apotheosis of life in its spiritual essence for which the speech by Rebecca at the close of Act I is a preparation. In addition, the scenes present an increasingly broad perspective of time and space. Act I, up to the time of the key passage by Rebecca, deals with the town in relation to its own history and geography; Act II, with the relationship between the wedding and the history and aspirations of Mankind in all ages; and Act III, with the relationship between life and eternity.

These relationships are expressed for the most part by the Stage Manager, either in his role as Stage Manager or as a character. In Act I, he gives the "facts" about the town; in Act II, he draws the parallel between physical nature and human nature and puts the wedding into the category of natural phenomenon. Both the earth and the people of Grover's Corners have grown older since Act I—three years before—but "Nature's been pushing and contriving in other ways, too: a number of young people fell in love and got married." Nature, he says, is interested in quantity—in propagation of the species—but there is something else in nature that is interested in quality. Just before the wedding he (as the Minister) says: "The real hero of this scene isn't on the stage at all, and you know who that is. It's like one of those European fellas said: every child born into the world is nature's attempt to make a perfect human being. Well, we've seen nature pushing and contriving for some time now. We all know that nature's interested in quality, too—that's why I'm in the ministry."

This humanistic affirmation of the dual—"higher" and "lower"—nature of men is given concrete, ironic enactment in the naive will to perfection expressed by Emily and George:

EMILY: I always expect a man to be perfect and I think he should be.
GEORGE: Oh . . . I don't think it's possible to be perfect, Emily.
EMILY: Well, my *father* is, and as far as I can see *your* father is. There's no reason on earth why you shouldn't be, too.
GEORGE: Well, I feel it's the other way around. That men aren't naturally good; but girls are.

The wedding, the central symbol of the fusion of nature's physical and spiritual purposes, puts those purposes and the will to perfection into a religious context. Yet the Stage Manager withholds judgment as to the value of the wedding: "I've married over two hundred couples in my day. Do I believe in it? I don't know." The cycle of life is filled as much with misery and pain as it is with happiness; and it always ends with death. The third act takes up this theme and presents it in action as the dead Emily, reluctant to quit life, observes her own funeral and begs to be allowed to relive one day of her life, her twelfth birthday, which the Stage Manager permits her to do. Having lost her life, she finds, while observing and taking part once more in daily events, that it is too great a gift for mortals to appreciate or understand. "Oh, earth," she cries, "you're too wonderful for anybody to realize you."

In this act, the Dead are seated on one side of the stage, while the funeral and scenes of daily life take place on the other. The intrusion of death here has been criticized as being inconsistent with the tone of the first two acts. John Mason Brown, for instance, felt it disappointing because the chill of death was "inescapable," its words were too colloquial, and its ideas too small. "The familiar aspects of living, dealt with so imaginatively in the first two acts, dwindle here into guesses unsupported by high imagination," Brown said. Emily's return was "touching," but the universality of the first two acts lost its "purity" in the third.[7]

It can be argued, however, that there would be a greater inconsistency if the words in the final act were less colloquial than they are in the first two. Although the chill of death is inescapable, it is precisely what brings the contrasting scenes of life to their highest emotional intensity. The action begins quietly in the cemetery and builds in intensity to Emily's climactic imprecation to her mother in the most moving lines in the play: "Oh, Mama, just look at me for one minute as though you really saw me. Mama, fourteen years have gone by. I'm dead. You're a grandmother, Mama. I married George Gibbs, Mama. Wally's dead, too. Mama, his appendix burst on a camping trip to North Conway. We felt just terrible about it—don't you remember? But, just for a moment now we're all together. Mama, just for a moment we're happy. Let's look at one another."

This moment is set against eternity; vibrant life, with all its joy and grief, happiness and suffering, is contrasted to passionless death. Emily can appreciate the value of life because she has lost it. From the vantage point of eternity she sees that it is largely wasted and that its tragedy lies in the failure of human beings to feel—as she does as she observes the scene of her twelfth birthday—the full intensity of each moment, good or bad, through the agency of consciousness, love. Her agonized realization of this sends her back to the Dead, where the moment and the human passions have no existence and are, therefore, not painful to contemplate.

Tragic waste, blindness and ignorance, failure to realize that even such a routine matter as greeting the milkman is a precious part of a priceless gift—that is the "discovery" the deceased Emily makes about life in Act III. But the presence of the Dead on stage with her has a mystical significance also. In contrast to Emily, who has just arrived among them, the Dead are indifferent to life on earth—or like Simon Stimson, whose life has been unhappy, contemptuous of it. While Stimson, Mrs. Soames, Mr. Carter, and Mrs. Gibbs still have their identity, the rest do not and will eventually lose it. The Stage Manager says of them at the opening of the act: "They're waitin' for something that they feel is comin'. Something important and great. Aren't they waitin' for the eternal part in them to come out clear?" All the problems and joys, the grief and happiness, and the love and indifference, it is suggested, are dissolved in the transcendent Whole: the perspective from which life is viewed in the last act is the "Mind of God."

A myth puts specific characters, actions, and themes into a microcosmic relationship with the universal forces that act upon and from within men; it draws together past and present; and it provides an analogy by which deep-felt needs, desires, aspirations, and fears of the individual become an expression of those of all men. The little New Hampshire town of Grover's Corners is Wilder's microcosm. His hero is human life itself; the universal forces acting upon it are Time, Nature, and Death; the forces acting from within it are Instinct, Love, Despair, and Apathy. Its scenes of daily life, love, marriage, and burial of the dead are the cyclical life-rituals of men and women in all times and places. The hopes and aspirations, the customs and habits, the happiness and misery its citizens think are so important—as Emily and George feel their marriage is important— are really not very important at all when considered in light of all the other human beings who experience the same things.

Through his presentation of Life in this mythic American village, Wilder renders the bittersweet truth that despite the unimportance of their lives in the larger scheme of things, the people continue, as George and Emily do on their farm, in the belief that what they do has significance; and yet, ironically, they never quite realize that because life is so short, and because it is all they have, they should live every moment as intensely and consciously as their hearts will allow. The mythic vision in *Our Town* carries the assumption that these humble, undistinguished people live their lives in relation to a pattern, a cycle, that ends in death and imposes upon them therefore a moral imperative to know that life is a precious gift not to be wasted or valued cynically. The beauty intrinsic to the patterns of their lives is interwoven with the pathos implicit in their failure to understand and achieve all that life has to offer. The moral order of which they are a part and of which they fall short is one in which love is the highest law. This Christian message is the purport of Emily's speech to her mother in Act III, when she begs Mrs. Webb to look at her as though she really saw her—with the consciousness that love engenders.

Regarded in the light of an assumed moral order of love, the presence of the Dead on stage in Act III receives added dramatic justification; for, while Wilder is not trying to show the "conditions of life after death," the Dead are, as the Stage Manager says, waiting for the "eternal part in them to come out clear"; and repetition of "Blessed Be the Tie That Binds," among other things, suggests that the moral order has a mystical basis. Moreover, the fact that Wilder borrowed the idea for the last act from Dante suggests that, like him, he intended his work to show that the love that animates and brings meaning to life is a manifestation of the cosmological order of things.

In this respect, T. S. Eliot's distinction between romantic and classical mysticism is apropos of *Our Town*. According to Elizabeth Drew, Eliot distinguished between "romantic" and "classical" mysticism by noting that in romantic mysticism the tendency is to substitute divine love for human love. In Dante, whose mysticism was classical, the effort was "to enlarge the boundary of human love so as to make it a stage in the progress toward the divine."[8] Enlarging the scope of human consciousness is Wilder's primary purpose in showing the disparity between the real value of life and the one of which the characters are aware. The audience does not feel any great concern for the outcome of the action since this is known from the beginning. It should feel, as Emily does, that failure to realize the value of life is essentially a failure to love every moment; and it should recognize that it is love which will be left after "the earth part burns away, burns out"—as the Stage Manager says of the Dead.

Our Town is thus a kind of religious festival—in accordance with Wilder's dramatic theory—celebrating Life. The Life it celebrates is the simplest and least pretentious imaginable; yet, as modestly as Wilder puts forth his view of life in *Our Town*, the play unquestionably captures and portrays the essentials of a mythic vision that ties life in his New England village to the "All, the

Everywhere, and the Always." It is a vision particularly satisfying to Americans who still cling to Whitman's ideal of an America that is a "nation of nations" drawing its moral impulses and values from a transcendent view of the inherent worth of the individual human being. Wilder loves his people despite their shortcomings (perhaps, even, partly *because* of them) and clearly intends that the audience should too. In making the little American town a mythical representation of civilized human life everywhere in all ages, he accomplished what he and Gertrude Stein conceived to be the main achievement of the literary masterpiece—the use of the materials of human nature to portray the eternal and universal residing in the collective "human mind." The theatricalist mode of presentation is so closely woven with the themes that it is an expression of them; and one feels compelled to say that *Our Town* could not have succeeded by any other means.

III   The Matchmaker

In his next play, Wilder turned theatricalism and farce into a satire about dramatic and social convention. *The Merchant of Yonkers* was a plea for a freer stage and a freer and fuller participation in life. Its first performance was at the Colonial Theatre in Boston on December 12, 1938, a little less than eleven months after the first production of *Our Town* at Princeton, New Jersey. On December 28, 1938, it opened in New York, where it had a short run of twenty-eight performances. It lay unused until Wilder revised it slightly, changed the title to *The Matchmaker*, and brought it out again in August 1954, in Edinburgh. From Edinburgh it went to London, where it began a successful run the following November 4. In October 1955, it was brought to Philadelphia, where it also succeeded; and when taken to New York, it enjoyed a run long enough to win "hit" status.

The Matchmaker doesn't differ materially from *The Merchant of Yonkers;* and it belongs, therefore, with the work of this earlier period of Wilder's career rather than with that after World War II. As Harold Clurman pointed out in his review of *The Matchmaker*, the failure of the earlier version and the success of the latter were probably owing to the difference in directors. *The Merchant* was directed by Max Reinhardt, for whom Wilder wrote it; and it failed, probably, because of what Clurman called the director's "unfamiliarity with American theatre custom."[9] *The Matchmaker* was

directed by Tyrone Guthrie, who by common critical consent kept
the action moving at the rapid pace it requires.

Wilder took much of the material for this play from Johann
Nestroy's *Einen Jux will er sich Machen* (Vienna, 1842). He calls it a
"free adaptation" of Nestroy's play, which was in turn based upon
A Day Well Spent (London, 1835), by John Oxenham. "One way to
shake off the nonsense of the nineteenth-century staging is to make
fun of it," he wrote in the preface to *Three Plays*. "This play
parodies the stock-company plays that I used to see at Ye Liberty
Theatre, Oakland, California, when I was a boy." Much of its
humor arises from the use of such old comic stage devices as mistaken identity, quick leaps from hiding places under tables,
characters dressed in clothes of the opposite sex, and people caught
in folding screens. It features stock characters and absurd situations
that develop into a conventional complicated plot. It has a
"villain," for instance, in the merchant Vandergelder, who tries to
prevent the marriage of a young couple—his niece Ermengarde and
the impecunious young artist Ambrose Kemper.

The action takes place in Yonkers during the 1880s and involves
the efforts of the principal characters, whose enjoyment of life is in
one way or another dependent upon Vandergelder, to "participate"
in life. In addition to Ermengarde and Ambrose, the main characters include Vandergelder's two clerks, Cornelius and Barnaby,
who go to New York in search of "adventure," and Dolly Levi, the
"Matchmaker," who pretends to make a match for Vandergelder
with a young, attractive woman (Irene Molloy) but actually makes
it for herself. Vandergelder's "sensible" behavior and values are the
obstacles in each instance to their free enjoyment of life, and the
plot consists in the attempts of these people to combat his life-
denying conventionality. His most formidable antagonist is Dolly
Levi, who is the arranger, the artist of life who follows no doctrine
except that of the full enjoyment of it and opposition to the conventional theories of "success" held by Vandergelder, to whom work
and money are life's highest values. She frankly and simply wants to
marry him for his money, but her ideas about wealth are in direct
opposition to his. She is determined to put Vandergelder's coins into
circulation so they can free others from habit, convention, and
isolation—for the enjoyment of life. She explains her economic
"philosophy" to Ambrose: "Money should circulate like rain water.
It should be flowing down among the people, through dressmakers
and restaurants and cabmen, setting up a little business here, and
furnishing a good time there."

When she has conquered Vandergelder, his unconditional sur-
render contains assurances that his money will be spent instead of
saved. Vandergelder is "sound" from the standpoint of conventional social values; for he has saved, worked hard, and been
cautious. He is the stolid, pompous "self-made" man who equates
the acquisition of riches and the exploitation of others with virtue
and "good sense." The clever Dolly turns the platitudes he lives by
to her own uses in such delicious bits of dialogue as the following:

VANDERGELDER: Mrs. Molloy, I've got some advice to give you about
your business.
MRS. LEVI: Oh, advice from Mr. Vandergelder! The whole city should
hear this.
VANDERGELDER: In the first place, the aim of business is to make a
profit.
MRS. MOLLOY: Is that so?
MRS. LEVI: I never heard it put so clearly before. Did you hear it?
VANDERGELDER: You pay those girls of yours too much. You pay them as
much as men. Girls like that enjoy their work. Wages, Mrs. Molloy, are paid
to make people who do work they don't enjoy.
MRS. LEVI: Mr. Vandergelder thinks so ably. And that's exactly the way
his business is run up in Yonkers.

Enjoyment of life requires nurturing of a vice as well as the virtues. The ne'er-do-well Malachi expresses this bit of wisdom:
"There are some people who say you shouldn't have any weaknesses at all—no vices. But if a man has no vices, he's in great
danger of making vices out of his virtues, and there's a spectacle.
We've all seen them; men who were monsters of philanthropy and
women who were dragons of purity. We've seen people who told
the truth, though the Heavens fall—and the Heavens fell. No,
no—nurse one vice in your bosom. Give it the attention it deserves
and let your virtues spring up modestly around it."
The clerks Cornelius and Barnaby are also in rebellion against
Vandergelder and what he stands for. Yearning for excitement and
resolving to go to New York for an "adventure," they blow up the
tomato cans on the shelves of Vandergelder's store and leave. They
are determined to have a good meal, to be "in danger," almost to
get arrested, to spend all their money (three dollars), and to kiss a
girl. Much of the best humor of the play consists in the attempts of
these two—and, later, Irene Molloy—to have a part in the excitement of life heretofore denied them by conventions that equate
"adventure" with foolishness. It is tender humor, a bit sentimental,

even a bit "heartwarming," but nevertheless very enjoyable. The hilarious scene in Act III, where Dolly twists Vandergelder's exasperation with her into a hinted proposal, is one of Wilder's most comical.

It is interesting that while this play first appeared during the depression and featured a conflict between a villainous "boss" and his exploited employees, it was utterly unproletarian; it did not present a "problem" for which social amelioration or reform was needed. The play says in effect that Vandergelder is a moral rather than a social problem. Like *Heaven's My Destination*, it proposes that a vigorous, robust spirit of humanism is the answer to materialism: that effective reform should begin with the moral improvement of individuals rather than with legislation. But the play is really too good-natured to command serious consideration of its humanistic propositions; and perhaps this is one reason it failed in the thirties. Furthermore, it lacks the bite of real satire; and, while there is some ridicule aimed at conventional notions of "success," the character representing it, Vandergelder, is so candidly, absurdly, and farcically "bad" that the seriousness of what he represents does not become apparent.

There is less claim to serious attention and contemplation in this play than in any of Wilder's other full-length works; and it should be enjoyed for what it is—a farce. The laughter it evokes at Vandergelder and the conventions he embodies is that of compassion for a fellow human who is unaware of his own foolishness and not that of bitterness or contempt. Wilder often used the phrase "make fun of" where "satirizes" might ordinarily be expected. The difference in terminology is relevant, for he seldom *satirizes*. He takes the more gentle way of viewing his people with mild irony, and he achieves a kind of spontaneous gaiety out of his depictions of human folly instead of a laughter of superiority and contempt. The result in *The Matchmaker*, which has had popular success on the stage and in the movies as the musical comedy *Hello, Dolly!*, is that we laugh at Vandergelder's absurdities without having to give much thought to their social or ethical significance.

IV   The Skin of Our Teeth

In *The Skin of Our Teeth* (1942) Wilder brought his theatricalism and humanism together most successfully with the comic spirit. His literary passion in the late 1930s and early 1940s was James Joyce, whom he was lecturing and writing about frequently,[10] and in *Finnegans Wake* he found many of the materials he needed to reaffirm those traditional human values that had once again been lost sight of as Europe plunged into World War II. *Skin* was written, as he said, in his preface to *Three Plays*, "on the eve of our entrance into the war and under strong emotion and . . . it mostly comes alive under conditions of crisis."

The first audiences had difficulty understanding the play, or were impatient with it in spite of Tallulah Bankhead's hilarious enactment of Lily Sabina; and Harrison Smith reported in the *Saturday Review of Literature* that there were empty seats during the last act of the performance he saw. But most of the critics understood it—early reviews were generally favorable—and Wilder received his third Pulitzer Prize for it.

But when Henry Morton Robinson and Joseph Campbell, who were working on their "Key" to *Finnegans Wake*, saw the play, they immediately recognized its similarity to the Joyce novel. They published a series of articles in the *Saturday Review* titled "The Skin of Whose Teeth?" in which they showed that the play drew heavily upon the *Wake* in themes, plot, characters, dialogue, and devices of presentation. They charged that the play was "an Americanized re-creation, thinly disguised," of *Finnegans Wake* and that the novel was "directly and frankly imitated, with but the flimsiest veneer to lend an American touch to the original features."[11]

Their evidence was indisputable, but many critics resented their insinuation that Wilder was guilty of plagiarism, and the argument that followed was nearly as fierce as the Michael Gold dispute twelve years before. George Jean Nathan, never favorable toward Wilder, not only applauded Campbell and Robinson but gave them his support.[12] Edmund Wilson, one of the few besides Wilder and Campbell and Robinson who understood Joyce's work at that time, wrote that while *The Skin of Our Teeth* deserved its success, it would no doubt suffer from comparison with *Finnegans Wake*.[13] Harrison Smith stated with some indignation that the question was not whether Wilder was a plagiarist, but whether he had "pulled a fast one on the public and especially those dramatic critics who received his play with mixed, but in some cases, wild enthusiasm."[14] *Time*, in spite of a generally unfavorable review of the play, maintained that Campbell and Robinson were "trying to make headlines out of footnotes, were confusing influences with imitations."[15] It quoted Wilder himself as saying that all he could do was suggest that those who were interested in the matter "read *Finnegans Wake* and make up their own minds."

Wilder subsequently acknowledged his debt to Joyce; and, except for Robinson, who renewed his charges and added others in an article in *Esquire* in March 1957, the borrowing was accepted by critics as a legitimate use of one author's material by another for his own distinctive literary purposes. Where Wilder borrowed, he usually gave credit to his sources; and he had used other sources besides Joyce in this play. For instance, he borrowed some of his ideas for comic stage effects (such as flying scenery) from Olsen and Johnson's slapstick *Hellzapoppin'*; and, while it might be reasonable to expect an author to acknowledge one source, it is less reasonable to ask him to acknowledge two. Moreover, he might also be expected to give credits to his own earlier works such as "Pullman Car Hiawatha" and "The Long Christmas Dinner" from which he borrowed almost as heavily as he did from Joyce.

Although, as Wilder himself said, the play was "profoundly indebted" to *Finnegans Wake*, Campbell and Robinson's charges were soon forgotten; but their discoveries about the relationships between the novel and play can profitably be retained. Joyce has been borrowed from heavily for some time in spite of Campbell and Robinson's indignation; and borrowing authors have seldom felt compelled to spell out the Joycean influence.[16]

Why Wilder found *Finnegans Wake* an agreeable source to borrow from is not difficult to understand, for much of its material and many of its themes were similar to those he had used in his own works prior to 1939, when Joyce's book appeared in its complete form. Wilder had already used a structure that showed the cyclical repetition of life through successive stages in "The Long Christmas Dinner" (1931). This structure and the historical theory it implied were similar to the circular structure of the *Wake* and to Giambattista Vico's cyclical theory of history which Joyce himself borrowed from. In addition, nearly all of Wilder's works previous to 1939 reflected the same assumption of dualism and the mystical resolution of the conflict between opposites which Joyce achieved allegorically in the *Wake* and borrowed from the renaissance Neo-Platonism of Giordano Bruno. Furthermore, Wilder had already employed the devices of amalgamating characters from myth, folklore, and religion and from literature and history in *The Cabala*, *The Bridge*, "Mozart and the Gray Steward," "The Flight into

Egypt," and "Centaurs" for the purpose of demonstrating comparable cultural developments. And his own anthropological studies in Rome in the early twenties led him to much the same view about the similarity of human cultures that Joyce derived from Frazer's *The Golden Bough*—though it is quite likely that Wilder had read and been influenced by Frazer too. Undoubtedly *The Skin of Our Teeth* is deeply indebted to the Joyce work, but much of its technique and content also have precedent in Wilder's earlier works. Wilder could legitimately claim a good deal more in the play as his own than Campbell and Robinson allowed.

The three acts of *Skin* involve the struggles of Mankind to survive the periodic disasters that threaten it with extinction: glacial invasion, flood, and war. The first act pits Man against Nature; the second, Man against the moral order; and the third, Man against himself. The acts are arranged to encompass successively smaller units of time: Act I embraces geologic time; Act II, biblical time; and Act III, the time of recorded history. These units of time are focused upon the lives of the Antrobus family of Excelsior, New Jersey. The Antrobuses are the "typical American family," but they are also the Human Family; and, during the course of the play, they relive the whole history of the human race, its origin, its fight for survival against natural catastrophe, its fall and redemption, and its wars. In this representation the Antrobus family is like Joyce's Earwicker family, but with this difference: The Antrobuses, as Americans, are shown by Wilder to manifest their relationship (or at least their conviction that the relationship exists) to human destiny in their everyday lives. Joyce has Earwicker dream the events in *Finnegans Wake*, and the difference is an important one in that it points up the fact that Wilder was doing more than simply dramatizing the Joyce novel for American audiences; he was using some of Joyce's materials to implement his own mythical vision of the American family life as a microcosm and to bring the weight of past human experience and values to bear upon this age of perpetual crisis.

As in *Our Town*, the tone increases in seriousness with each act. In Act I, an Announcer—roughly the technical equivalent of the Stage Manager in *Our Town*—relates the news of the world as shown on lantern slides projected on a screen and declares that "The sun rose this morning at 6:32 a.m." The tone is comical, but this introductory scene relates the Antrobuses to present-day America, to biblical time, and to the Ice Age and prepares for the play within the play that follows. The play he introduces is repeatedly interrupted by characters stepping out of their roles and into others as actors: the actress who plays Sabina expresses her dissatisfaction with her role and with the play itself; actors become ill and have to be replaced by stage hands; the actor who plays Henry Antrobus has his own psychological problems and breaks down in the middle of a scene with Mr. Antrobus. In all these interruptions a Stage Manager appears from behind the curtain to try to keep the action moving. This comic theatricalism is abetted by such *Hellzapoppin'* burlesque antics as flying scenery and by the presence on stage of a dinosaur and a mammoth. Aside from its own comic effects, this material—understandable by the "greater number"—directs attention to the ideas behind the actions and the characters.

The characters are all allegorical figures on three levels: as Americans, as biblical figures, and as universal human types. Antrobus—the middle-class American, Adam, and the "father pilot" of the human race—has the general weaknesses and virtues of humanity in general of all times. The basic fact about him is that he does not change much from year to year or from one period of history to another; and his problems are also much the same in every age. He is always on the brink of a disaster caused either by natural forces outside him or by inner conflicts, but he manages to survive by the "skin of his teeth." His wife is at once the American mother, Eve, and the eternal mother. While Antrobus is at his best rational and needs reasons for survival, she acts from instinct and guards her family "like a tigress." She is anti - intellectual and narrow (". . . I'd burn ten Shakespeares to prevent a child of mine from having one cold in the head"); but in spite of humiliation by her philandering husband and the eternal wicked woman (Sabina) and of disaster she remains constant in her determination to save her family. She is both simple-minded and mysterious; and the force that makes her like a tigress appears to be instinct but is actually the secret of life itself. In Act II she throws a bottle with a letter in it into the ocean. In the letter, she says, "is written all the things a woman knows."

The two Antrobus children, Gladys and Henry, represent, respectively, Antrobus' hope for human perfection and proof that his hope can never be fully realized. Henry, who bears the red ochre emblem of Cain and is constantly at odds with the rest of the family, including Sabina, is the allegorical figure of evil. Antrobus' struggles with him represent enactment of the principle of dualism. Lily Sabina, the Antrobus maid, is also evil, but in a less fixed and absolute sense; for her sins are generally household or venial sins. She is the fainthearted maid on the American-family level of the play; but she also becomes, variously, the Semitic mythological figure of Lilith (the evil, wifely spirit); Miss Fairweather, to whom Antrobus turns when no disaster threatens and he doesn't need help and guidance; Sabina, the "robber of the Sabinerennen"—as told by Livy—whom Antrobus "raped . . . home" to insult Mrs. Antrobus, as she says in the free verse passage in Act I. Lily, who provides much of the comedy in the play, has all the weaknesses of her kind: lack of conviction; lack of courage before adversity; vanity; ignorance of everything above the level of appetite; prudishness; and self-righteousness.

These main characters are Americans who, like the people of *Our Town*, have hidden in their daily lives the key to the destiny of the human race. Antrobus' daily work at the office is a project of as great importance to him, it is implied, as the invention of the alphabet, the number system, and the wheel. When he pinches the maid, he commits a moral transgression which (though comical because of the discrepancy) is parallel to the rape of the Sabines by the men of Romulus. When his wife tells their daughter Gladys to pull down her skirt, she is preserving the morals of the race; but, when Antrobus kisses the bathing beauty, he is corrupting them.

Conflict in the play is dialectical; for ideas are pitted against one another in opposite pairs. Antrobus himself does not change; only his ideas do. The comic-serious tone increases tension between the ideas with irony. As time-present and time-past are put into the eternal present, the action and characters attain the allegorical level. Lily Sabina stands in dialectical opposition to Mrs. Antrobus, Henry-Cain to Antrobus, and, again, Henry-Cain to Gladys. In opposition to all of them in Act I is the glacier, which represents natural disaster—a phenomenon for which no cause is indicated; it unites the human family, good and bad, in the common cause of survival. The unity and the determination to survive, however, come only after Antrobus decides that the race is worth saving. He undergoes an inner struggle of doubt and despair when Mrs. Antrobus refuses to give shelter to Homer and Moses and when he sees his own evil in Cain. His decision to survive comes when Moses and Homer (Judge and Professor, Hebraism and Hellenism, Sweetness and Light) are saved and when Gladys announces that in school she had an "A" in "Conduct" and had recited perfectly in assembly (again, sweetness and light).

The humanistic affirmation of the play is clear enough, and again Wilder's humanism ends in faith. The act ends with Gladys reciting the opening lines of Genesis and with Sabina calling to the audience to help save the human race. The dramaturgy, then, is theatricalist and presentational, the thematic treatment allegorical, the themes religious-humanistic. The question remains, however, as to whether form, style, and themes come together in a successful fusion.

Act I shows survival to be a matter of will and courage based upon faith in human and religious values, but Act II depicts it as a matter of acceptance of moral responsibility. The allegory is more directly religious than in Act I, for it affirms the principle of individual responsibility in Old Testament terms. In Act II geologic, biblical, and modern times are telescoped again, as they are in Act I, with an Atlantic City convention which is shown concurrently as an ordinary businessmen's convention; as a convention of the "Ancient and Honorable Order of Mammals, Subdivision Humans"; and as the biblical world just before the Flood. The convention is a sort of combined Sodom and Gomorrah and Vanity Fair where pleasure and irresponsibility run rampant. The end inevitably is destruction, either through the self-destructive nature of its pleasure-seeking or by a God of Justice.

The central symbols of the act are the bingo parlor and the fortune teller which signify, respectively, chance and destiny, or circumstance and fate, or accident and predestination. The right (moral) choice, it is implied, reduces the extent to which chance, accident, or circumstance governs life. The Conveeners have their "chance" to abandon their pleasure-seeking and choose the right way, but they fail. Antrobus, who nearly fails, is saved only at the moment of the Flood when he leaves Lily Sabina-Fairweather behind and accepts his responsibilities to his "family"—Mankind. Absent from this act are the humanistic-allegorical figures of Act I—Homer, Moses, the Muses. The moral content of Act II is in a primarily religious context—Judeo-Christian in its emphasis upon retribution and redemption and, of course, its basis in Genesis. The vision in Act II is one of man paying heavily for his moral transgressions and follies. Torn between his responsibilities to his family and his desire for the easier life of indulgence, Antrobus wavers but redeems himself at the last moment; but his fellows at the convention, refusing to heed the warning of the apocalyptic Fortune Teller, follow the course of pleasure and die for it.

Act III resumes the religious-ethical themes of the first two acts and shows Antrobus courageously rebuilding after war. He still has Sabina and Cain to contend with and is weary and disheartened; but he again makes the decision to accept his responsibility to the human family. Once more, his guidance and justification are in his books—Spinoza, Plato, Aristotle, and the Bible. His attitude is one of resignation but hope:

Oh, I've never forgotten for long at a time that living is struggle. I know that every good and excellent thing in the world stands on the razor-edge of danger and must be fought for—whether it's a field, or a home, or a country. All I ask is the chance to build new worlds and God has always given us that. And has given us

(Opening the book)

voices to guide us; and the memory of our mistakes to warn us. Maggie, you and I will remember in peacetime all the resolves that were so clear to us in the days of war. We've come a long ways. We've learned. We're learning. And the steps of our journey are marked for us here.

The play does not imply that the world should adopt American ideals and mores. What it says is that hidden in American life are the weaknesses that have hindered and the moral and religious values that have assured man's survival since the beginning of civilization. Wilder's historical view here rejects the theory of progress; for the circular form, with Lily Sabina repeating her opening lines at the very end of the play, indicates that history will follow a similar cycle. But Antrobus is not the hopeless prey of endless cycles of disaster; he says: "We've come a long ways. We've learned. We're learning." He can do nothing about natural disasters, and evil (Cain) is so much a part of him that he knows he can't escape it; but he can and does keep evil under control; and, with courage and acceptance of moral responsibility, he can eliminate disasters which are of his own making. With faith in his better self—as defined in the great works of his cultural heritage—and in God, he will continue to survive and even to triumph although other creatures perish.

This message is the serious side of *The Skin of Our Teeth;* but Wilder's humanistic temperament sees a comical, ridiculous facet of the good and bad in men—and in the American—as well as a serious one. The other side of the good Mrs. Antrobus is the prudish one. The other side of Adam-Antrobus is the vulgarian who makes his entrance in Act I with: "I'll be scalded and tarred if a man can't get a little welcome when he comes home. Well, Maggie, you old gunny-sack, how's the broken down old weather hen?—Sabina, old fishbait, old skunkpot.—And the children,—how've the little smellers been?" The theatricalism—which is both comic and serious—is intended in part to offset the didacticism and conventionalism of the themes. But it sometimes does its job too well, for it tends to overwhelm the themes. Moreover, the mixture of comedy and seriousness does not always come off successfully. One might ask, for example, how the author can have his Fortune Teller tell about "shameful things" and "total destruction" one minute and expect his audience to take those warnings seriously in light of the comic handling of Antrobus' seduction by Sabina which follows.

Furthermore, the play lacks the effective objective correlative that *Our Town* has in its repeated view of the ordinary life of the town; nor does it have the compelling concrete demonstration of its propositions. By Act II of *Our Town* Emily and George, in spite of the fact that they are generalized, are powerful emotional referents; in *Skin* the referents are weak because they are abstractions from the beginning; and their actions lack, therefore, the basis in common experience that gives concreteness to the themes of *Our Town*. The humanistic theme of sweetness and light in the first act, for example, which is demonstrated by Gladys' announcement that her conduct and performance at school were "perfect," is intended to illustrate the operation of those great human values in everyday American life and to indicate their importance by making them the deciding factor in Antrobus' decision to fight for survival; but the actual effect of this demonstration of the great by the small is to reduce the former without raising the latter to the point of convincing affirmation.

The same result also comes of having the Muses, Homer, and Moses (who are "typical New York out-of-works") join in singing "Tenting Tonight." The effect is not, as intended, to raise the American camp meeting to an affirmative humanistic level, but to make comical the symbols used seriously in Act III. Again, in Act II the moral degradation of Antrobus is handled with such lightness of tone that the "shame" of it is not convincing—it looks more like a minor indiscretion than a threat to the moral fiber of the human race. In Act III, the moral weakness of Sabina and the "evil" of

Cain are confronted by Antrobus, who admits his own evil and moral weakness but affirms his survival again on the basis of values he has inherited and maintained. These values, which can be identified generally as the search for ideal truth and beauty (Spinoza), moral order and responsibility (Plato), belief in the potential divinity of man (Aristotle), and faith in God (Genesis again) are intended to be taken with full seriousness in Act III. But, after the almost cavalier treatment of the Antrobus affair with Sabina in Act II, the recitations of passages from the philosophers in Act III seem inappropriately serious.

The Skin of Our Teeth is Wilder's most complete and direct dramatic expression of his theory of the relationship between the American and "destiny," as well as the most complete achievement of his theatricalist theories. If the play proves anything, it is that theatricalism and allegory can be a dangerous mixture unless leavened with some degree of concrete fact; they must have some basis in real experience. Literal and allegorical meanings, comedy and seriousness, theatricalism and realism (almost totally lacking) are inadequately balanced to make the themes convincing and provide a unified vision of a faltering, absurd but noble mankind surviving not only because of but in spite of itself. *Our Town* is sufficient proof, therefore, that Wilder's thematic purposes are best served by the presence of at least enough slice-of-life presentation to put his themes in direct relation with objective experience.

Perhaps it is not possible to do successfully what Wilder undertook to do in *The Skin of Our Teeth*—to relate a single family to the "All, the Everywhere, and the Always"—without making the family convincing first in concrete, partly realistic terms. To do so, as he does in *Our Town*, is a more effective method of drawing the audience into the action in order—in ritual or festival fashion—to formalize its deepest ethical and religious convictions. The theme of the play is really less optimistic than the comedy and theatricalism lead one to believe; for the play says at one level that there is little we have ever been able to do about periodic catastrophes except to cling to our best spiritual achievements and faith in God. There are a good many laughs in *The Skin of Our Teeth*, which may very well be the best thoroughly theatricalist work of the American theatre;[17] but it seems to demonstrate also that religious humanism and burlesque are not very compatible dramatic ingredients.

Yet one hesitates to try to say anything final about *Skin*. Time has been good to it, and it seems likely to outlive many better made plays. Wilder's statement that it comes to life best during times of crisis probably accounts for its great success in Germany and Poland after World War II. It is basically a tribute to man's indomitable will and an expression of faith; and if, in an era of perpetual crisis, it instills the kind of faith it demonstrates—especially in Act III—it will have to be judged as much by the authenticity of its message as by the quality of its dramaturgy.

CHAPTER 5

Existentialism and Humanism

I N 1942, the year *The Skin of Our Teeth* was first produced, Wilder enlisted in the Intelligence Corps of the Air Force as a captain and spent the next three years in the United States, North Africa, and Italy; he was discharged in 1945 as a lieutenant-colonel. As an intelligence officer his special concern in the battle against dictators was with information and resistance from within enemy territory—a fact which may have turned his thoughts to the subject of absolute power and freedom. It is also likely that the Mediterranean atmosphere drew his mind to the classic instance of absolute power and civil resistance to it that culminated in the assassination of Julius Caesar in Rome on March 15, 44 B.C. In addition, the loss of a friend, Roman poet Lauro De Bosis, who was killed while attempting to organize a resistance movement against Mussolini, made the fact of resistance and the question of living and dying for principles of a personal one. These factors, plus an interest in the philosophy of crisis that had come out of the resistance movement in France, seem to have been the main causes of the writing of *The Ides of March*, one of the best American novels of the post-World War II period.

I The Ides of March

Absolute power and resistance to it in Caesar's Rome is the subject matter of *The Ides of March*, but Wilder's purpose is not simply to retell the history of Caesar's overthrow by the Roman aristocracy in order to draw parallels with events during World War II. His Caesar has almost nothing in common with Mussolini or with Hitler except that he is a dictator. Unlike the fascist dictators, he is a hero who holds Rome under his command because he is resolute and decisive and because, unlike his antagonists, he is wholly committed to action. He is the most powerful man in the world because he has put aside all illusions about universal meaning and benevolence, turned to advantage the isolation which is the condition of all men, and responded decisively to all situations demanding decision. A man of responsibility, Caesar contrasts to his arch-antagonist Brutus, who, guided by ideals and systems of philosophy, is irresolute, irresponsible, and weak. *The Ides of March* is, therefore, an ironic turnabout on the subject of absolute power and freedom; for it is the dictator Caesar who, being free, stands as a symbol of the greatness, nobility, and power of the man who has discovered his humanity through both the suffering and the triumph of total "engagement." The fall of such a man is tragic, and Wilder's Caesar attains real tragic stature.

Wilder's interest in the existentialist philosophy of Sartre after World War II can be readily explained. A humanist like Sartre, Wilder had always maintained the position that ethics have to be defined in an exclusively human context without reference to religious or philosphical preconceptions. Although his humanism, unlike Sartre's, ended in religious faith, he was careful to keep moral considerations separate from religious doctrine and insist, as Sartre did, that any meaningful prescription for human conduct has to be grounded in experience rather than *a priori* philosophical or religious ideas. This view was implicit in *The Bridge*, for instance, where he maintained that any meaning that life was to have would have to come from individuals themselves and that the first step in the creation of a meaningful existence was commitment with love to responsibility for others. His interest in Sartre's philosophy was that of a believer and a moralist in the affirmations of a nonbeliever. His Caesar is the embodiment of the Sartre hero; and Caesar's tragedy is in part the inevitable tragedy of such a character.

In his "Existentialism and Humanism," Sartre declared that among the major tenets of existentialism are the propositions that existence precedes essence, that man is "nothing else but that which he makes of himself," that he is responsible for all his fellowmen, that he is "condemned to be free," that there is no reality or morality except in commitment to action, and that there are no *a priori* values. Therefore, the "moral choice is comparable to the construction of a work of art"; for, like the artist, man is forced to create his own moral world.[1]

Wilder's Caesar has become and remained ruler of Rome because he has acted in accordance with these assumptions. His loneliness as ruler of Rome represents man's isolation in the universe and in the world. But that isolation gives him heroic potential. Having directed the fortunes of Rome from war to peace, he now wants to build a greater Rome; but he must first answer the question of what its purpose will be. Since he rules Rome and since it rules the world, he, in effect, directs the destiny of the world, is responsible for all his fellowmen, and is charged with defining the purpose of life. He writes to his friend Turrinus: "The projects which now visit me . . . involve certain elements about which I am not certain that I am certain. To put them into effect I must be clear in my mind as to what are the aims in life of the average man and what are the capabilities of the human being. Man—what is that? What do we know of him? His Gods, liberty, mind, love, destiny, death—what do these mean?"

Committed to life and "the obligations of living," he is impatient with philosophy. "I have regarded philosophy with impatience," he tells Turrinus in a letter, "as a tempting but fruitless exercise of the mind and as a flight from the obligations of immediate living." His own experience has convinced him that any ethical position must be based upon response to situations that demand vital decisions—upon what Sartre calls "engagement." He says: "The first and last schoolmaster of life is living and committing oneself unreservedly and dangerously to living; to men who know this an Aristotle and a Plato have much to say; but those who have imposed cautions upon themselves and petrified themselves in a system of ideas, them the masters themselves will lead into error. Brutus and Cato repeat liberty, liberty, and live to impose on others a liberty they have not accorded to themselves——." There can be no freedom, he maintains, except in responsible action; in the acceptance of the necessity of making a moral choice for which the individual alone is responsible and which in its enactment affects his fellowmen. Responsibility is the highest morality; and the actress Cytheris observes of Caesar that he is essentially a teacher and that "the essence of what he has to teach is moral, is responsibility."

His ethical conviction that man is compelled to be free and that "Life has no meaning save that which we may confer upon it" derives from his metaphysical belief that man is alone in a universe that does not know he exists—a world Sartre held to be meaningless. But while he is quite sure it is meaningless, he is not certain; and he is constrained from issuing an edict he has written abolishing religion because an element of doubt remains in his mind. "Some last hesitation arrests my hand," he tells Turrinus;

and, unable to commit his conviction to action, he remains in doubt.

Caesar is thus a counterpart of the man of faith. Where the believer's faith is troubled by doubt, Caesar's disbelief is qualified by uncertainty. He is unable to make a final statement about the absence of any "mind behind our existence" because of the possibility of mystery in four realms of his life and in life generally: love, great poetry, his epilepsy, and his position as leader of Rome. "If I acknowledge the possibility of one such mystery," he says, "all the other mysteries come flooding back." These realms offer possibilities of mystery because they are paradoxical; they may spring from the lowest in man's nature, but Caesar has observed or felt in them the highest human experiences. For example, love may be an instinct, as it is in Clodia Pulcher; or it may be a passion in which the self is forgotten, as it is with Catullus. The great lyrics Catullus writes for Clodia may spring alike from love and hatred, good and evil. Caesar's epilepsy may be simply a physical disorder, yet during his seizures he has a vision in which he seems to "grasp the fair harmony of the world." And, finally, he observes that while he has attempted, perhaps from wholly selfish reasons, to shape Rome to his idea and "give it a sense," he is not entirely sure that he is not actually an instrument of destiny.

Suggested in these mysteries is a teleological option to the existentialist assumption that the universe is without meaning; that is, the possibility that while the initial causes of love, great poetry, his epilepsy, and his power may be easily enough explained in human terms, the final causes may reside in a meaningful, ordered universe—in God. The metaphysical irony basic to *The Ides of March* consists in Wilder's substitution of "Unknowable" for Sartre's "meaningless" in describing the operation of the universe. Wilder presents a very convincing portrayal in Caesar of the existentialist ethical and metaphysical assumptions of Sartre; but he then undermines the certainty behind those assumptions by affirming the presence of mystery, which compels a tentative attitude toward them. The recognition that life is essentially a mystery sets into motion Caesar's inquiries into the meaning and nature of life; and the applicability is clear from the epigraph Wilder chose from a passage in *Faust* and glossed as "Out of man's recognition is fear and awe that there is an Unknowable comes all that is best in the explorations of his mind,—even though that recognition is often misled into superstition, enslavement, and overconfidence."

This statement is in general the philosophical basis of the book. But while *The Ides of March* is a philosophical novel, it is a *novel* and not a work of philosophy. Its philosophical framework is grounded in the lives—both inner and outer—of the characters; and, considering the difficulties inherent in the imaginary-document mode of presentation Wilder uses, the characters are remarkably individual and alive. The thematic tensions that derive from the conflicts in Caesar's mind and grow between him and his antagonists include those of belief and disbelief, necessity and choice, tyranny and benevolence, and freedom and responsibility.

These tensions are related by means of three types of documents that convey the life of Rome and Caesar's ethical ideas and metaphysical speculations. The first type includes letters, reports, directives, and pamphlets which are of direct and immediate interest and which convey the flux of Roman life. These documents provide the action of the narrative; for they have the conflict, tension, and immediacy of scenic presentation. They generally lack reflection and summary for they are official papers, orders by Caesar, or incitements to action against him; the letters provide a kind of dialogue of action between such correspondents as Brutus and Servilia, Clodia and Catullus, and Caesar and Cleopatra.

The second type of document functions technically as summary narration which tells what has happened and perhaps conjectures about what will happen. These documents, like the first type, describe the major characters and relate their actions; but, in contrast to the first, the writers usually offer their own comments about the events and the people they write about and the authors are themselves minor characters who are only marginally involved in the main course of events. Examples of this type are the passages from the Commonplace Book of Cornelius Nepos and the letters of his wife Alina to her sister; in these such incidents as Cleopatra's arrival in Rome and Catullus' death are related.

The third type of document is primarily reflective in nature. Most of the documents in this group consist of Caesar's letters to Turrinus, but they also include Cytheris' letters to Turrinus. These epistles contain most of the ethical and religious comment in the book, and they reveal Caesar not only as the private man and student of life but also as the ruler. The sources of reflection in these letters are for the most part the incidents reported in the documents of the first type; and, while these letters tend to be essayistic, they avoid the kind of essayism so objectionable to Jamesian crit-

ics—where the author speaks as author—because they are written
by characters who are steeped in the life they comment on and
reveal themselves as they write.

All these documents are arranged into four chapters organized according to theme and time; and each succeeding chapter embraces
and extends the previous one. Each ends with a misfortune for
Caesar—a foreshadowing of the final disaster of March 15. The first
begins with a report to Caesar by the College of Augurs about the
behavior of the birds of prophecy, and it ends with Caesar's epilep-
tic seizure after the first assassination attempt and during Clodia
Pulcher's party; it covers the month of September, 45 B.C. The second chapter opens with a letter, dated August 17, from Servilia to
Pompeia about the expected arrival of Cleopatra, and it ends with
the incident in which Antony and Cleopatra are found in an em-
brace. The third begins with Caesar's letter of August 9 to the president of the College of the Vestal Virgins requesting purification of
the rituals, and it ends with the profanation of the rites by Claudius
Pulcher and with Caesar's divorce from Pompeia because of her
part in it. And the final chapter opens with Servilia's letter, dated
August 8, to Brutus asking him to return to Rome to help depose
Caesar; and it ends with the assassination. With each of the first
three chapters ending badly for Caesar, the feeling of inevitability is
established.

The vision Wilder achieves is one in which the people of Rome
have a direct relation with human destiny. Since Caesar's fate is
known in advance, attention is focused from the beginning upon
the question of its causes—a strategy (similar to that of *The Bridge
of San Luis Rey*) which compels the reader to give close attention to
the details of character and action in order to find the reasons for
the disaster. The question that commands the reader's interest is:
"What sort of person is Caesar and what factors in his own personality and in the personalities of the people of Rome brought
about his assassination?"

The most palpable factor in Caesar is the self-destroying nature
of his belief in total commitment to action. Having achieved
freedom for himself through the responsibility gained by
"engagement," he has forgotten that others—also "condemned to
be free"—will seek to test their freedom through decisive commitments to action. Furthermore, deprived of the responsibility
Caesar has assumed, they will commit themselves to irresponsible
acts. Thus Catullus launches an irresponsible campaign against

him; and Brutus, not really understanding freedom, assassinates Caesar in its name. The actress Cytheris says of Caesar: "It is not that, like other tyrants, he is chary of according liberty to others; it is that, loftily free himself, he has lost all touch with the way freedom operates and is developed in others; always mistaken, he accords too little or he accords too much." He has forgotten that other men have to explore the limits of liberty before they can assume responsibility. Ironically, he has so shaped Rome to his own idea, that, when he fells, his Rome must tumble also.

Another factor in Caesar that leads to his downfall is his isolation as a ruler. Much of the sympathy the reader feels for him arises from awareness of the discrepancy between the private Caesar—who shows real compassion and solicitude for his invalid friend Turrinus, tolerance and concern for Catullus, and grief for his dead daughter—and the public one who refuses to permit Cleopatra to bring their child to Rome. The discrepancy between the two Caesars is the paradoxical result of his conviction, on the one hand, that because man is alone in the universe he must act under that assumption and of his personal inclination, on the other hand, to dispel his loneliness with acts of love and kindness. "The condition of leadership adds new degrees of solitariness to the basic solitude of mankind," he tells Cleopatra.

Her reply indicates her awareness of the extent to which his isolation as ruler is self-imposed and excessive: "You have described to me the solitude of a ruler. A ruler has reason to feel that most of the approaches made to him are colored with self-interest. Is it not the danger of rulers to increase this solitude by ascribing to others that motivation alone? I can imagine a ruler turned to stone by such a view of his fellow men and turning to stone all those who approach him." She adds that ". . . you have, indeed, created for yourself a solitude that is excessive even for the ruler of the world."

The fact that metaphysical and ethical necessity in part governs the public Caesar but that he himself has chosen to accept isolation and responsibility establishes him as a tragic representation of the human condition. In living by the laws of the universe, he represents the condition of man; and, because he *chose* to do so, he is tragic. But the real essence of his tragedy is his excess in both isolation and responsibility, which has detached him from the aristocracy and generated contempt on his part and hostility on theirs. Caesar the dictator is respected but not loved; for his physician Sosthenes says of him: "Caesar does not love, nor does he inspire love. He diffuses an equable glow of ordered good will, a passionless energy that creates without fever, and which expends itself without self-examination or self-doubt."

The private Caesar, whom these people never know, is revealed primarily in his letters to Turrinus; and in the contrast between what the public Caesar has to be and what the private Caesar is lies the irony that evokes a feeling of inevitability and of pathos at his death. While the letters to Turrinus contain Caesar's metaphysical and ethical reflections, they also reveal his emotional depth. His urbane and sophisticated style and his loftiness of thought are softened by feelings that are unexpressed but grounded in the tone of the letters. Turrinus, having lost his arms and legs in war, lives in seclusion on Capri. He is a sufferer, to Caesar a fellow-sufferer, whom he respects because Turrinus has been schooled in affliction and has gained from it a wisdom and courage nonsufferers lack. The letters to him are characterized by warmth and complete confidence, and they reflect Caesar's innermost feelings and thoughts. They convey, therefore, the various facets of his character: the reflective Caesar; the Caesar whose love for Rome is deeper than his love for its citizens; the Caesar—reminiscent of Shaw's—who is amused at the follies of men (and particularly by the religious follies of the women of Rome and the calculating ambition of Cleopatra); and the angry and disgusted ruler who is contemptuous of the motives and principles of his fellow Romans. Yet withal they reveal a man of dignity and nobility, of great understanding and sympathy for those whom life has hurt. Drawn without sentimentality, he is a powerful figure; and by the end of the book he has gained the full stature of a tragic protagonist. He is Wilder's most complex and convincing character.

Of the other characters in the book, the women emerge most clearly and effectively and make the greatest impact upon the life of Rome and upon Caesar. Except for Caesar none of the men is delineated sharply. Cicero's letters tell more about Caesar than about Cicero, and Catullus' letters reveal more about Clodia than himself. But the letters of the women define distinctly and often ironically the personalities of their writers. Deeply involved in matters of everyday life, these women have a tremendous influence upon the fortunes of Rome through their power over the men. The notorious Clodia Pulcher incites Claudius Pulcher to profane the rites of the Good Goddess; and she inspires Catullus' great lyrics to "Lesbia," poems that move Caesar so profoundly that he is constrained to call great poetry one of the real mysteries in life and to observe that Catullus' strange, unrequited passion for Clodia is an instance of the mystery that is love. Servilia pens the letter that first puts the idea of resistance into Brutus' mind—she is the woman whom Caesar has given in younger days "the rose-colored pearl that she wears so religiously at every celebration of the Founding of the city." And from the Queen of Egypt—passionate, impulsive, capricious, loving a Caesar who comprehends her better than she knows herself and loving him because Egypt's welfare depends upon him—come the letters and the state documents showing her in all her phases: the offended mother, the proud queen carrying the dignity of a nation and a dynasty with her, the playful mistress, and the distressed and misunderstood one.

Influencing consciously or unconsciously the men and institutions of Rome, these women act upon their own feelings and intuitions rather than upon reflection; and their power is that of emotions rather than of intellect. Practical above all and steeped in the trivia of everyday, they have great spiritual potential which could be realized, as Caesar observes, if directed into useful human activity instead of into such absurdities as primitive religious rites. "Let each woman find out in herself her own Goddess," he tells Turrinus and expresses what religious ritual should mean. Yet the women are generally more effectual than the men because, like Caesar, they commit themselves to action.

The document mode of presentation permits Wilder to get both inside and outside his characters without the "editorial presence" of an omniscient author. The characters define themselves by what they say and do or are reported to have said and done; and from the interplay of conflicting sentiments, viewpoints, and reports about a number of subjects and actions arises a vision that has the complexity, intensity, and paradoxes of life itself. With this method the danger of the philosophical novel is avoided, for the life presented is not merely a contrivance to illustrate ideas but has immediacy. While Caesar in general embodies the free man in existentialist terms, his part is not unnatural to him in his capacity as a leader. Moreover, existentialism by its nature precludes fitting life to a scheme of ideas; for it requires instead that action rather than ideas be the source of reflection.

The Ides of March remains Wilder's best novel. Complexity of vision and intricacy of organization place it above any of his other fictional works, and none of the characters in his other novels has the emotional and intellectual completeness that Caesar has. Although it is not likely to be so widely read as *The Bridge*, it is a better novel in terms of craftsmanship, and while both *The Bridge* and *The Eighth Day* have a number of memorable characters, none has the dimensions of a great tragic protagonist, as Caesar does. Although the documentary method precludes the dramatic effect of direct presentation of incidents ("scenic" presentation), it makes up for this loss by enabling the author to convey objectively not only his characters' minds but their actions. In the intricate picture he presents of the interplay between the outer and inner lives of these characters, Wilder achieves the most completely satisfying vision presented in his works of fiction.

II   The Alcestiad

Like *The Matchmaker*, *The Alcestiad* had its premiere performance in Edinburgh, where it was presented in 1955 under the title *A Life in the Sun*—a title imposed upon it by the producer and one with which Wilder was not happy. It failed in Edinburgh; but subsequent performances in Switzerland, Austria, and Germany achieved notable critical and popular success. The German version, was performed before enthusiastic audiences in Hamburg, Germany, in the fall of 1958 and received reviews that a jubilant Wilder remarked he could have written himself.

The legend of Alcestis and her sacrifice interested Wilder for some time before he wrote *The Alcestiad*. In *The Woman of Andros*, the hetaira Chrysis, while reflecting about "why we suffer," had observed that the answer would come some day when "I shall be among the shades underground and some wonderful hand, some Alcestis, will touch me and will show me the meaning of all these things. . . ." In this novel the hoped-for Alcestis was Christ, whose birth brought religious sanction to the moral and ethical principles Chrysis and Pamphilus already embraced.

Wilder also related the moral to the religious in the Alcestis legend in *The Ides of March* when he had Catullus recite the "Lost Alcestiad of Catullus"—Wilder's own version—at the Pulcher party just after the first attempt to assassinate Caesar; and this narrative is the basis for Act I of *The Alcestiad* in which it brings a religious dimension to the legend by having Alcestis seek to renounce life in order to serve Apollo. Wilder not only added it to the main incidents of the great Greek original by Euripides but also added a third act and a satyr-play to give religious and metaphysical meanings to the action. The result was an allegory in which self-sacrifice is viewed in its ethical, religious, and metaphysical implications.

The Alcestiad retains, however, much of the flavor of Greek drama. Constructed like a Greek tetralogy, it has three serious parts and the satyr-play. It also has in the Watchman a chorus, for he has the same role of the Stage Manager in *Our Town* in that he interprets the action, relates antecedent events, and reports the consequences and effects of the action upon the citizens in general. Although the second act includes the major incidents—Alcestis' sacrifice for Admetus and her resurrection by Hercules—of the Greek original, Wilder, as he usually did when he borrowed, altered the structure, myth, and characters to suit his own purposes. For one thing, *The Alcestiad* covers the thirty years from Alcestis' marriage to Admetus to her death; and the first act occurs on a day ten years prior to the action of the *Alcestis* and the third act takes place twenty years after her death and resurrection. For another, Wilder changed Admetus from the coward of the Euripides version to a beloved king and husband who is unafraid of death, who enjoys the blessings of divine grace, and who is not unworthy of Alcestis' sacrifice. And Wilder's Alcestis and Hercules, unlike their forerunners in *Alcestis,* consciously try to find meaning in their lives.

In maintaining the characters, the setting, and the main incident of the original Greek version, Wilder followed the way of Cocteau (*The Infernal Machine*) and Sartre (*The Flies*) rather than that of T. S. Eliot, who so transformed the Alcestis legend in *The Cocktail Party* that he had to point out the relationship. Wilder's reason is clear and simple: the Greek myth in its own dress gave him—as the Oedipus myth and the *Oresteia* gave Cocteau and Sartre—the materials to put his characters in direct relationship with the gods; that is, the laws of the universe. That relationship, as Wilder depicts it, is quite different from the relationships shown by Cocteau and Sartre, whose gods are either malicious or alien toward men and whose protagonists gain humanity through suffering at their hands or freedom through rebellion against them. The picture Wilder offers is, however, of a God of love (Apollo) who tries to make himself felt and understood by men but is unable to do so without human help. Wilder's mankind is helpless before circumstance until shown the way to humanity—and thence to divinity—by one who commits herself wholly to the highest expression of love—self-sacrifice.

The Alcestiad is an existentialist allegory portraying the mystic's pilgrimage. It presents directly the religious affirmation that was only suggested as an option to Caesar's skepticism in *The Ides of March*. Wilder himself said: "On one level my play recounts the life of a woman—of many women—from bewildered bride to sorely tested wife to overburdened old age. On another level it is a wildly romantic story of gods and men, of death and hell, of resurrection, of great loves and great trials, of usurpation and revenge. On another level, however, it is a comedy . . . about the extreme difficulty of any dialogue between heaven and earth, about the misunderstandings that result from the 'incommensurability of things human and divine.' "[2] Each of the first three acts presents variations on the theme of self-sacrifice as an expression of love; and the levels of love and self-sacrifice are worked out in an ascending order to culminate finally in an epiphany and mystical union in Act III.

The vision is mystical in its portrayal of the union of Alcestis and Apollo in divine love; but it is existential in its illustration of the necessity of complete commitment to life in human love and self-sacrifice as the first step towards divine grace. This existentialist theme is the "lesson" that Apollo tells Death he wants to teach. The theological picture is that of a God-Creator not entirely in control of the human life he has set in motion because he has given men freedom. Not understandable to men, he tries to find means of communicating with them; but, the more he tries, the more he torments them. Death says to Apollo in Act I: "Leave these human beings alone. . . . They will never understand your language—how can they? The more you try to say something, the more you drive them distraught." Because men have freedom, they suffer the torment of living in a world in which the gods give them no aid, in which they are subject to the forces of chance and necessity, and in which their lives are without meaning except insofar as they give them meaning.

In each of the first three acts Alcestis makes a commitment to love which appears to have no value beyond itself. The greater her suffering and the more complete her commitment, the more absurdly meaningless they seem to be from the standpoint of her own welfare. But her purely human, moral commitments are indispensable first steps to the divine: they must be made without hope of reward. The young Alcestis of Act I refuses to marry Admetus because she wants to live "in the real" by devoting her life to God; any woman, she maintains, can have a family, devote her life to it, and finally sink into the grave "*loved* and *honored* but as ignorant as the day one was born" of ". . . why we live and why we die—of why the hundred thousand live and die. . . ." She wants a "sign" from Apollo that he exists and that life has a meaning. "It is time we asked for certainties," she tells her maidservant Aglaia; but just when she is ready to leave Pherai to serve Apollo at Delphi, the prophet Teiresias arrives and announces that Apollo has been commanded by Zeus to live among men for a year. Apollo has chosen Admetus' kingdom, Teiresias declares, and comes as one of four herdsmen who are waiting outside the city gates. Alcestis' first reaction is that of hope; but disillusionment with the possibility of a direct sign from Apollo comes when she sees that the "divine Teiresias" is now vulgar, mean, bitter; he is condemned like the Wandering Jew to live without hope of death.

Her disappointment in the blind prophet is followed by loss of hope for a "sign" from the drunken and dirty herdsmen who—though individually endowed with remarkable powers of cure, poetry, and vision—lack the moral consciousness that signifies divinity. Alcestis' despair at her discovery contains a hint of atheistic existentialism: "Then we are indeed miserable. Not only because we have had no aid, but we are cheated with the hope that we might have aid . . ." Her naive hopes for "certainties" shattered, she turns to a commitment of her "whole self" in love for Admetus. The first stage of her pilgrimage is, therefore, to turn away from asceticism and renunciation to "engagement" in life itself and to the creation of her own meaningful, moral existence. Her vow to live her life for Admetus comprises choosing a situation for herself: She now exists in the life of another, who likewise depends upon her for his existence. In telling Admetus she will live for him as though at any moment she might have to die for him, she unconsciously affirms her moral freedom—she is free of the bondage of trying to live according to preconceived notions about the will of God.

In Act II she puts her moral freedom to its highest test. Told that Admetus has been wounded accidentally by one of the herdsmen and must die unless someone will die for him, she decides to give her life to save him. As in Act I, her commitment is unqualified and is a "work of love"; for she insists that her sacrifice be made without

consideration of self. When the herdsman who has wounded
Admetus begs her to let him make the sacrifice and thus expiate his
sin, she refuses to allow it, saying ". . . you would do it imperfect-
ly; Admetus will be completely well only if I can completely die for
him, give all myself to death. You wish to die, yes—but not for love
of Admetus. You wish to die in order to lift the burden of that crime
from off your heart." Commitment to death represents, therefore,
the second step in her pilgrimage.

In Act III the scope of the action broadens to show the universal
effects of Alcestis' commitments. Thessaly becomes a microcosm; its
people, Mankind. A plague has gripped the city, and its citizens are
in despair. The barbaric King Agis has usurped the throne and put
Admetus to death. Alcestis has been spared but reduced to ser-
vitude; and, of her children, only Epimenes, who has fled, survives.
But despite Alcestis' misery and suffering she—when Epimenes and
his friend Cheriander return to Thessaly to kill Agis—dissuades
them and turns their efforts to helping rid the city of the plague. In
spite of her losses, she also tries to give courage to Agis, whose
daughter Laodarnia has just died, by convincing him life has other
values besides love. "Love is not the meaning," she tells him. "It is
only one of the signs that there *is* a meaning. It is only *one* of the
signs that there is a meaning." While she does not spell out the
other "signs," her act of kindness towards her malefactor Agis and
her acceptance of responsibility for ridding Thessaly of the plague
demonstrate what she means.

In existentialist terminology, Alcestis becomes a kind of spiritual
legislator for mankind. Like Orestes in Sartre's *The Flies*, she is an
exile in her own land; like all other human beings, she is alone in
the universe; and she is, therefore, at once free and responsible. But
unlike Sartre's atheistic view of Orestes, who becomes human in his
defiance of the gods and acceptance of the burden of his people's
sins, Wilder's Alcestis becomes both human and divine through
finding and realizing herself in others. By turning Epimenes and
Cheriander from assassination to constructive effort, she in effect
unites her people against the common enemy and conquers it. In
the epiphany that closes Act III, Apollo affirms the final union of
the human with the eternal and the transcendent—the mystical fusion of the human soul with the principle of Life or with God or
Light.

The existentialist, mystical nature of the ethical, religious, and
metaphysical themes that culminate in the epiphany in Act III is

unmistakable. By her actions Alcestis puts the eternal love of God into being in time through her own existence (and therefore in the lives of all who experience her act); and she achieves the paradoxical truth of the absurd: The eternal exists in the temporal, a condition which Kierkegaard conceived to be the basis of Christian faith. Alcestis' spiritual union with Apollo at her death represents the final achievement of her "eternal self." In the terminology of Kierkegaard, her pilgrimage is the process of "becoming." She becomes what she does. Giving herself completely to acts of love, sacrifice, and mercy, she becomes the incarnation of those qualities and thus establishes communication with Apollo.

Considered metaphysically, Alcestis' sacrifices have the effect of defeating the forces of chance and necessity which govern the universe. This theme is stated in the satyr-play, "The Drunken Sisters," where Apollo tricks the three Fates—Atropos, Clotho, and Lachesis—into sparing Admetus but learns that, while he can outwit them, he cannot control them. If Admetus is to live, Lachesis tells Apollo, someone else must sacrifice his life with freedom of choice: "Over such deaths we have no control. Neither Chance nor Necessity rules the free offering of the will."

In the process of "becoming," Alcestis has the help of Apollo. In Act III Apollo tells Death, "I am finding that language which is received as a secret in the heart of each one, and yet which is addressed to the billions." He has also helped Admetus to yoke the lion and the boar in order to win the hand of Alcestis. And he helps Hercules bring Alcestis back from death. Preparing to descend into Hades, Hercules prays to Apollo to "Put into my arm a strength that's never been there before. You do this—or let's say: you and I do this together. And if we can do it—let everybody know that a new knowledge has been given to us of what Gods and man can do together."

Wilder's meaning in this passage bears a strong resemblance to the mystical existentialism of Nicholas Berdyaev, which holds that man participates in God's creativity and that the moral act is one of co-creation which leads ultimately to mystical union of the human and the divine. Alcestis' triumph over necessity and chance, over the injustice of Agis, and over death itself by her acts of love, sacrifice, and mercy parallels in a general way the theological precepts of Berdyaev, who maintains in his *Dream and Reality* that each moral act of love, mercy, and sacrifice helps to bring an end to the power of hatred, cruelty, and selfishness in the world. Every moral act, Berdyaev holds, concurrently diminishes necessity, enslavement, and inertia; and it brings to actual existence "a new 'other' world, where God's power is revealed in freedom and love."[3]

Although there is no extrinsic evidence that Wilder was influenced by Berdyaev, it is not unlikely that he was because the mystical nature of Berdyaev's existentialism effects the identification of the religious life with ethics and the divine in the human which Wilder tries to establish in this play. The act of co-creation by Alcestis and Apollo is a change in the order of things in which Alcestis' moral actions are expressions of God's will: They bring the promise of a "new, 'other' world." In Act I, Apollo announces the change when he says to Death: "You live in the dark and you cannot see that all things change." That the change, the victory over Death in Act II, is partly the result of Apollo's efforts is indicated in their dialogue in Act III, where Death says to Apollo in reference to Alcestis' resurrection: "You broke the ancient law and order of the world. The law—since men were created and Hell was established—that law that the living are the living and the dead are the dead." And, finally, the theme that a new, religious-moral meaning has come into the world is expressed by Apollo when he says to Death: "You are one of the few that can understand that when I talk to *one* [Alcestis], I am also talking to the innumerable."

The Alcestiad thus has a religious existentialist theme. Yet one feels while reading the play that its meaning is too often revealed by characters who are self-consciously philosophical. Direct expression of ideas and interpretation of action not only render it didactic at times but preclude full realization of its potential of dramatic power. Because the action is overburdened with ideas, the play needs in the first two acts a strong human conflict. Cocteau and Sartre brought fresh meaning to the myths they used largely because they transformed the just Greek gods into tormenters and tyrants under whom human beings suffer or rebel against—or both. Wilder's play, following generally the Greek pattern of the protagonist's departure from and gradual reconciliation with a god of wisdom, carries less force and conviction. Absence of conflict also makes Alcestis' victory in Act III less impressive than it might be because it is won with less struggle than it seemingly requires. She suffers no real soul-searching before committing herself to her choices. Her dark night of the soul in Act I is brief, and no real doubts disturb her decision to turn away from Apollo and live solely for Admetus. Because of these factors, she lacks the depth and complexity a greater struggle might have given her.

The mystical nature of the theme is, however, responsible for the absence of conflict; for the tendency of mysticism to resolve conflict through love renders conflict avoidable—and desirably so. Thus Alcestis, the mystic, discourages Epimenes and Cheriander from their plan of violence against Agis and directs their efforts to helping rid Thessaly of the plague. Thus, too, the struggle over the sacrifice in Act II is not a struggle over *whether* to die for Admetus (as the argument between Pheres and Admetus in *Alcestis* is, by contrast) but over *who* will do it—Aglaia, the Herdsman, or Alcestis; and, although Alcestis decides she will do it because she most loves life, and, therefore, will be making the greatest sacrifice, the fact that it *is* a great sacrifice to her is not evidenced by any visible suffering on her part. The power of love is so great that no agonizing struggle is necessary for such a sacrifice as Alcestis makes. This is what these actions imply. There is little conflict among the characters, therefore, until the last act; and even then Alcestis succeeds in preventing violence.

If one conceives of drama as in imitation of actions involving conflicts between strong protagonists, *The Alcestiad* undoubtedly is weak; for the conflicts are among characters attempting to impose value and meaning upon their lives through devotion to and sacrifice for others. The real source of conflict lies in the dialectical tension between faith and the facts of life. From the beginning suspense is built around the questions of how Apollo and Alcestis will bridge the great gulf between the human and the divine, and of how Death—the darkest, most compelling fact of life—will be conquered. As in *The Bridge*, the facts do not justify faith. Alcestis' reward for her sacrifice appears to be the wretchedness of slavery; his labors, Hercules complains to Admetus, do not seem to justify any belief in his own divinity; and the four herdsmen, though endowed with such powers as those of the healer and the poet, do not appear to have the moral qualities requisite to divinity—or even to human dignity.

Yet all have the divine within them—and the potential to realize it, as Alcestis does in her acts of love, self-sacrifice, and mercy. Typically, Wilder puts the burden of courage and faith upon the individual as he faces the unpleasant facts of life. As the Watchman says: "The facts remain the same . . . It is ourselves that change . . . we pray to the gods not to alter the circumstances of life but to give us the condition wherein to view them." Alcestis attains this "condition"; and, if we could wish that she had come by it and sustained it with more difficulty, we must recall that Wilder's intention is not to make the circumstances of life appear too formidable. His intention—in which he succeeds—is to show also that it is within the power of every individual to rise above despair through exercising the great moral and ethical principles of love, self-sacrifice, justice, and mercy—and gaining thereby the help of the gods.

Alcestis becomes, therefore, a symbol of what all men and women can do and be. Though she lacks complexity, she develops as few of Wilder's dramatic characters do. Her development is toward an inner serenity and moral strength which give her the will to carry on in the face of adversity and provide her with the basis for a sound faith. From a naive belief that the "real" can be found in renunciation of life, she achieves the realization that reality is an inner thing and that the first place to look for God is within herself. Although she is one of Wilder's better characters from the standpoint of development and growth, Alcestis' main weakness is that of the play as a whole: She conforms too much to the idea of the mystic. Moreover, because she confronts loss of faith, death, and injustice with love, sacrifice, and mercy, she becomes sentimentalized at times and seems to make her sacrifices with too much self-conscious martyrdom.

The Alcestiad seems destined for greater success as an opera than as a stage play. Wilder apparently had an opera in mind when he wrote it, and as with "The Long Christmas Dinner"—first performed as an opera in 1961 in Mannheim, Germany—its mystical themes, emphasizing harmonies, find their most effective expression through music. Like Whitman's poems "Out of the Cradle Endlessly Rocking" and "When Lilacs Last in the Dooryard Bloom'd," which were set to music by Hindemith and Roger Sessions, respectively, *The Alcestiad* is built around recurring themes and variations, and resolves its conflicts in a climactic, mystical affirmation that lends itself to the emotional pitch achieved by an aria. Like Whitman, Wilder loved music and was familiar with its forms. He was also no doubt aware that a number of his plays, by their very nature, were admirably suited to musical adaptation. It is likely that the future will see more musical adaptations in the manner of *The Alcestiad*.

CHAPTER 6

Final Entries

A FTER the premiere of the operatic version of *The Alces-tiad (Die Alkestiade)* in Frankfurt, Germany, early in 1962, Wilder resolved to get away to a place remote enough to provide him with privacy and uninterrupted time to write a novel that had been taking shape in his mind. On May 20, he left Hamden and drove to the little southeastern Arizona town of Douglas, where for the next eighteen months he worked on *The Eighth Day*.

The five months prior to his departure for Arizona were very satisfying ones. The success of *Die Alkestiade*—which was set to music by Louise Talma—was preceded in December 1961 by an equally successful opening in Mannheim, Germany (the Germans always had an especial fondness for Wilder), of *The Long Christmas Dinner*, for which Paul Hindemith composed the musical score and translated Wilder's libretto into German. Audiences in Germany were enthusiastic and reviewers generous in their praise. In New York, José Quintero's production of *Plays for Bleecker Street* opened on January 11 at the Circle-in-the-Square Theatre, bringing to the stage three of Wilder's one-act plays, "Someone from Assisi" from a projected cycle, *The Seven Deadly Sins;* and "Infancy" and "Childhood" from *The Seven Ages of Man*.[1] Quintero's skillful direction and the theatre-in-the-round staging brought favorable notices. Reminiscent of Wilder's earlier one-acts in their ethical-religious themes and theatricalism, they found a responsive audience in Bleecker Street, though their run was a brief one. Climaxing those months of heady success and recognition was an invitation to read from his writings on April 30 as the special guest of President Kennedy's cabinet in Washington, D.C., for a program—one of a series sponsored by the Kennedy Administration to honor outstanding writers, artists, and performers—titled "An Evening with Thornton Wilder."

Other honors were to follow in succeeding years: the United

States Presidential Medal of Freedom in 1963; the National Medal
of Literature in 1965; the National Book Award (for *The Eighth
Day*) in 1968. But in May 1962 Wilder knew he had to get away and
be free from all distractions, gratifying as they were, if he was to do
any serious writing. Shortly after the opening of *Die Alkestiade* he
told a reporter in Frankfurt that he was "heading out into that
Arizona desert to be a bum for two years. As soon as I get back to
the States," he said, "it's going to be two years without neckties,
without shoelaces and without cultivated conversation." When the
citizens of Douglas, Arizona, saw him, as they often did, he was
usually wearing both a tie and shoelaces, but the quiet, uncomplicated life there provided the necessary antidote to the
sophisticated and glamorous world of theatre and celebrities, for
The Eighth Day was to be about obscure people in some of the least
glamorous places imaginable. Like *Our Town* it would focus on two
small-town families but would take place variously in a dismal
Illinois mining town; Chicago; Hoboken, New Jersey; a mountain
village in Chile; and a number of other out-of-the-way places. He
checked in at the 170-room Gadsden Hotel in Douglas—where
miners, cowboys, cattlemen, and prospectors gathered in the
spacious lobby—and began to write.

I   The Eighth Day

Wilder's most serious, comprehensive, and penetrating examina-
tion of American life, *The Eighth Day* conveys once more his long-
standing conviction that because Americans are free from the
traditions, the confinement to place, and the forces of history that
shape the lives of people in other lands, they have a special
relationship to the universal and timeless truths of the human race.
In many respects it is his capstone work, for it brings together into a
complex microcosmic portrait the themes, characterizations, story
and plot designs, and dramatic tensions recognizable in earlier
works; but it has a richer narrative texture and a more inclusive
social context than any of his previous novels. The title suggests a
new beginning, the first day of a new week, a new and better period
of time when the human race was "entering a new stage of
development—the Man of the Eighth Day," but we soon learn that
the title is ironic, for the setting and the action immediately belie
the notion that the new twentieth century would bring a better day
for America or the human race.

The portrayal of American society, as seen in the dreary mining town of Coaltown, Illinois, is less than flattering; indeed, it suggests a civilization in decay, and in fact we are told that Coaltown fades away with the exhaustion of its mines a few years after the end of the story. Cheerless, class-burdened and exploitative, Coaltown is controlled by absentee-owners who care nothing about either the people their company exploits or the ugliness of the scarred, blackened landscape it has destroyed. Dehumanized by its detachment from the lives of the people of Coaltown, the company is a metaphor for the soulless economic aspects of society whose spiritual bankruptcy has produced defeated, empty employees and a desolate industrial wasteland. Yet out of that sordid atmosphere emerge, like flowers from a dungheap, individuals and groups whose capacities for love, generosity of spirit, and courage provide the basis for hope, and our interest centers on their struggles to surmount the adversities imposed upon them by their environment and by fate.

A number of recognizably Wilderian techniques show themselves. As in *The Bridge*, a catastrophe—the killing of Breckenridge Lansing and the arrest of John Ashley for murder—initiates the narrative. Two closely connected families provide the focus of the action, which begins and ends in a small town, calling to mind the Webbs and Gibbses and Grovers Corners, though with differences that become obvious in the opening pages of the prologue. And in the manner of *The Ides of March*, the story moves forward and backward in time, from the date of the murder—summer 1902—and traces the lives of the Lansing and Ashley families. The events occur within a framework of geological, anthropological, and historical time, reminding us of a similar device in *Skin*, and suggested parallels between persons in the novel and characters from the Classical past recall hints of the same order in *The Cabala*. Lacing the narrative together and charging it with suspense is one of Wilder's favorite fictional strategies, that of investing an obscure, tragic human incident with mystery and tracing its causes, taking us into an intricate web of circumstances, personal relationships, character motivations, and philosophical speculations that in turn generate further, more complex mysteries about life.

The narrative strategy of *The Eighth Day* resembles that of *The Bridge* in directing our interest to the characters and their responses to the conditions the disaster imposes upon them. From our initial curiosity about the identity of the killer and the details and causes of Ashley's escape (both questions, in the best mystery-story fashion, are answered at the end), we are led to the complex motivations and relationships of the characters, whose lives contain the significant issues of the story as well as the maze of reasons behind the murder and escape. We know that Ashley is innocent, because we are told so in the prologue, and by the time the two mysteries are unraveled we are persuaded that the murder and escape were not only plausible but well-nigh inevitable. Yet while the mysteries of the plot are resolved, those raised in the prologue are intensified by the lives of the characters. What hereditary and environmental factors lay behind the fate of each, what "gifts and talents, and destiny and chance" can be detected? Wilder poses the old questions: "Was there a connection between the catastrophe that befell both houses and [the] . . . later developments? Are humiliation, injustice, suffering, destruction and ostracism—are they blessings?"

Arrested for the murder of Breckenridge Lansing at a family picnic while target-shooting, Ashley is rescued by several men, who conceal their identity and their reasons, in a daring and carefully planned scheme that frees him but separates him forever from his family. We follow him to New Orleans and then to South America, where, bereft of his family ties, he grows in sympathy and understanding through his contacts with a cross-section of people in the cities, mountain villages, and mining towns where he hides and changes his name. As a "man of faith," he undergoes a spiritual journey as he moves from one place to another in the Andes, and as an engineer, he restores meaning to his life through bringing his knowledge into the service of others. He rebuilds a dilapidated chapel, repairs the plumbing and constructs shelves in an orphanage, restores and improves school and hospital buildings. Work, creative work directed toward making life better for others, gives meaning to his life once more and brings him a measure of happiness again. A practical man, Ashley has always directed his efforts toward constructive ends, and a latent, unconscious idealism has given his work a creative cast. In Chile, he gains increased moral consciousness through contacts with María Icaza, "midwife, abortionist, *maga*, teller of fortunes, interpreter of dreams, go-between, exorcisor of devils"; with Dr. MacKenzie, managing director of the copper mine who has "read the Bible in Hebrew, *The Book of the Dead* in French, the *Koran* in German"; and with Mrs. Wickersham, proprietor of the Fonda hotel whose three interests are "her hospitals and orphanages; good company and good talk at her dinner table; and her reputation for knowing everything that's going on in the Andes." All three are flawed in various minor ways, but all contribute to Ashley's spiritual growth.

As a man of faith, Ashley embodies political as well as moral and religious implications. His origins are humble, his gifts and talents inherent but inexplicable, his instincts noble and generous, his understanding limited but capable of improvement. He and his children are the best American democracy can produce, and they are the best hope for the human race. But Wilder's hopes for the future are considerably dimmed by his Calvinist sense that the power of their counterparts is formidable and their lot is almost by definition a very difficult one. Though none of the characters is oversimplified—indeed, the complexity of characterization is remarkable—there is no mistaking the fact that the basic conflicts of the novel are waged between secular saints and sinners, the Elect and the Damned, the renate and the reprobate. None is wholly good or bad, but they all have characteristics that identify them as one or other other, and all define themselves by the manner in which they use their capabilities for doing good or ill to others.

The power of the faithful—Ashley, his son Roger and daughters Lily and Sophia are the major ones—is moral; it expresses itself in dedication to others who are in need, in the alleviation of suffering, in self-sacrifice, in beauty (Lily becomes a famous singer), in using one's native gifts (Ashley is an inventor, Roger becomes a journalist); in creative work. In contrast to the inner, individual strength of the faithful, that of the life-deniers is economic, legal, and exploitative. Breckenridge Lansing, resident manager of the mines in Coaltown, is a genial, hand-shaking, patriotic, God-fearing young Babbitt who "belonged to every lodge, fraternal order, and association that the town afforded" and was easily brought to tears by vows of fraternal loyalty, devotion to God, and love of country. Hypocritical, shallow, materialistic, unimaginative, and incompetent in his work, he is dissolute, sensual, negligent—a failure as a husband and as a father. He is all appearance and public image, and is inwardly corrupt. He represents the enormous economic, social, and puritanical moral power of the establishment; and Coaltown, a grimy, depressing wasteland scourged by poverty and social stratification, symbolizes the achievements of him and his kind.

By moving the story to New Orleans, Chile, Chicago, and

Hoboken, New Jersey, Wilder emphasizes the ubiquity of such types. Ashley is pursued in Chile by Wellington Bristow, a heartless hunter of escaped convicts who carries a "rat list" of those wanted by the law and who, like Lansing, represents the sinister, depraved forces of a society chiefly concerned with profits and losses. In Hoboken, we go back in time to the early years of Ashley's wife, Beata, and see the joyless, lower-middle-class existence of her Dutch parents, with their moral orthodoxy, snobbishness, social conventionalism. They are Philistines whose Sunday-school proprieties, careerism, and respectability stifle the creative impulses and free spirit. Like John Ashley's own parents, they resign themselves "to the knowledge that life is disappointing and basically meaningless" and aspire to nothing higher than the esteem and envy of their community, the appearance of contentment, and a spurious moral superiority. But, on the other hand, we also see the independent Ashleys ("indubitably . . . Americans"); unbound by conventions, they and the Kellermans—John's maternal ancestors—were free spirits, for good and ill, and the opposites of Beata's people. Whatever their weaknesses—and they were numerous—they are preferable to their counterparts, who live by received forms, inherited formulas, or their egos, and are predictable, fundamentally dull, and contemptible.

Those who live by conventions, and the ugly, materialistic society they conform to, form a backdrop to the dramas enacted by Wilder's secular elect, whose lives contain the stuff of his affirmations about the democratic man and woman, the possibilities for democratic culture, and the hope for the future of civilization. They have the Protestant virtues of responsibility, industriousness, and independence; they give purpose to their lives by discovering and developing their native gifts or talents and putting them to constructive use; and they have a great capacity for love, self-sacrifice, and dedication to the alleviation of suffering. We see John Ashley's son Roger refusing to succumb to adversity, as he becomes a famous journalist in Chicago and devotes his energies to exposing the plight of the poor as well as helping his mother and her family back in Coaltown. We observe Ashley's daughter Lily, a free spirit who blithely ignores Victorian notions of sexual propriety, as she singlemindedly pursues her career as a singer; and we follow the resourceful child Sophia as she contrives means of getting money for the fatherless, indigent Ashley family—and destroys herself in the process. Each is unique, but they are also representative of the best America—and humanity—has to offer, Wilder tells us. He gives us a gallery of minor characters to demonstrate their universality: the cultured and sensitive seamstress, Miss Doubkov, an immigrant from Russia who understands and helps Lansing's troubled son George become a great actor; the old Indian Deacon of the Covenant Church, a wise man of God whose congregation engineered John Ashley's escape in return for a good deed he had earlier performed for them; and a host of others, believers and nonbelievers from various walks of life, who in small or large ways make life better for others. They are the faithful, the hopeful, the charitable. They comprise the natural aristocracy.

As usual, Wilder has nothing to say, directly, about the United States as a political entity; there are no politicians or government institutions involved in this or any of his other works. This is partly a result of the fact that his main interest is moral rather than political or social, but it is also a result of his concern with the universal and timeless rather than the merely local or temporal aspects of life. For him the family is, has been, and will probably continue to be the basic social unit, for he sees the family as the main custodian and purveyor of the best values of civilization. But the "nuclear" family is the family of the human race in little, and—as we see in *Our Town* and *Skin* as well as in *The Eighth Day*—its main purpose is to teach the lessons necessary for commitment to the human family. In practical terms, this means creative involvement with others in everyday life—not with the idea or reforming them or society but with the will and courage to help make their way smoother.

Such is the moral, the religious, message of the book. Near the end of the story the old Indian Deacon points to Coaltown and says to Roger Ashley: "They [the people] walk in despair. If we were to describe what is Hell it would be the place in which there is no hope or possibility of change: birth, feeding, excreting, propagation, and death—all on some mighty wheel of repetition." We may assume that he speaks for Wilder when, quoting Isaiah, he praises those individuals who "Make straight in the desert a highway for our God," that is, those persons who, like John Ashley, act upon the best within themselves to bring beauty, truth, and joy to their fellow creatures. As for the United States of America, the old man says cautiously that it is possible that "this country which so greatly wronged my ancestors" is "singled out for . . . a high destiny," that of offering hope to those in despair.

Wilder's final view toward his homeland is, like Walt Whitman's, one of hope mixed with foreboding. The possibilities of a great democratic culture exist, and they may be realized if those endowed with superior sensibilities and intelligence prevail and put the best that has been thought and said into active use; otherwise, the United States, like Coaltown, will have its brief day and pass, spiritually and physically spent, into history as a failure. The power and effects of Breckenridge Lansing and his kind are obvious enough to prevent any undue optimism and put to rest any residual belief in progress. The human race, Wilder says, doesn't change much from one period to another; civilizations rise and fall in accordance with which values they adhere to—the humane values inherited from the cultural past, or the hard, materialistic ones descended from the primal ooze.

Like Emerson, Channing, and Parker a century before, Wilder combines a transformed Calvinistic consciousness of the human potential for evil with a belief that men and women have the freedom to act upon nobler impulses. In this regard, he belongs to what R. W. B. Lewis has called the "Party of Hope," for despite reservations that became increasingly compelling in his final serious, critical work, he never portrays a human situation as hopeless as long as there is a will to act. Wilder frequently uses the image of a tapestry to suggest that history has a design; his people, especially those with superior moral or intellectual endowments, always have the choice of being weavers as well as integral parts of the fabric.

Though *The Eighth Day* is Wilder's most ambitious work of fiction, it is by no means free of defects. Most notable is the annoying Wilderian moral self-consciousness that all too often takes the major characters to the brink of priggishness or pretentiousness, or both. And the frank depiction of Coaltown as a microcosm sometimes affects the credibility of both the town and the characters by placing attention excessively on their universality or typicality: an old problem for Wilder's readers to cope with. The characters, we feel, do not really need outside help from the author to define them, and we could do without so much of his interpretation.

Yet the novel as a whole surmounts its weaknesses and is Wilder's most impressive attempt to address the fundamental moral issues of the twentieth century, when the values of the Judeo-Christian and Classical traditions have sustained their most devastating assaults by industrialism, Freudian psychology, state paternalism, the loosening of family ties, the depersonalization of human relationships, and the steady loss of meaningful connection with the past. Few writers in this century have undertaken such a Herculean task; fewer still could have undertaken it—lacking Wilder's combination of intellectual sophistication and narrative skill; only the best—Yeats, Joyce, Mann, Eliot—among those writing in this century have done better.

II   Theophilus North

Though surely not by design, Wilder's literary works show a certain symmetry. He began with two collections of short plays (*The Angel That Troubled the Waters* and *The Long Christmas Dinner*) and two episodic novels (*The Cabala* and *The Bridge of San Luis Rey);* then during his middle years—the thirties, forties, and fifties—came a novel set in ancient Greece (*The Woman of Andros*), a novel and three plays (*Heaven's My Destination, The Merchant of Yonkers, Our Town, The Skin of Our Teeth*) set in America, and a novel (*The Ides of March*) and a drama (*The Alcestiad*) set respectively in ancient Rome and Greece. The final decade and a half of his life almost duplicated the twenties, with two more series of short plays (*The Seven Deadly Sins* and *The Seven Ages of Man*) and two more episodic novels (*The Eighth Day* and *Theophilus North*). The last two novels differed from the first pair in being set mainly in the United States, while the first two were placed respectively in Rome and sixteenth-century Peru. One has to be impressed by Wilder's range. Within the entire corpus of his works is a variety of genres, forms, settings, and characterizations unmatched by any other American writer; indeed, it would be hard to think of another writer anywhere or at any time who could match his versatility, which evidences his studied and deliberate mastery of forms.

Nevertheless, varied as his works are, they all bear his unmistakable stamp, and this is nowhere more true than in his last novel. In fact, *Theophilus North*—his only work except for his first novel, *The Cabala*, to be told entirely in the first person—carries the imprint not only of Wilder the author but of Wilder the man as well, to the detriment of its art. As in *The Cabala*, the narrator relates his experiences with a number of individuals he meets and becomes involved with during a few months' stay in the city—Rome in *The Cabala;* Newport, Rhode Island in *North*—where the action takes place. He has just resigned from his teaching job at a boys' preparatory school much like the

Lawrenceville School where Wilder himself taught in the 1920s. En route to Maine in the spring of 1926, he passes through Newport, where (as Wilder had done) he had served in the Coast Artillery during World War I, and decides to stay for the summer. He keeps a journal from which, fifty years later, he draws the materials for the sketches in the book.

Like most other first-person narratives, this one reveals the character of the story-teller as well as of the people in the story. In order to make his living in Newport, North gives tennis lessons and language instruction to children of the well-to-do who are there for the summer months, and he reads from Classical works of literature for older people who hire him. He explains that he is tired of teaching at the boys' school but doesn't want to be a full-time writer, either; he is chiefly interested in becoming "far more immersed in life" than having a profession or career allows. He must work for a living, but he wants to do it on his own terms and at times suitable to himself, and thus leave himself free to be involved in the life around him. He admits that he is "to all appearance cheerful and dutiful, but within . . . cyncial and almost totally bereft of sympathy for any other human being" except the members of his own family. He therefore finds a kind of spiritual therapy in getting involved with individuals who need his help.

North finds "adventures" in his involvements—we are reminded of the clerks in *The Matchmaker*. In one episode he cleverly heads off an ill-conceived elopement between a society girl and a high-school athletic coach; in another, he shrewdly brings back to an active life a wealthy retired diplomat who has been kept a semi-invalid for years by his future heirs; in yet another, he cunningly thwarts a group of counterfeiters. He is in great demand by some Newporters and is thoroughly despised by others, but once involved in their lives he becomes a manipulator in their best interests, usually helping free someone from a physical, emotional, or psychological condition or an idea or misconception that holds that person in bondage and prevents his or her full enjoyment of life.

North's nearest literary relative is George Brush, in *Heaven's My Destination*. Like others among Wilder's do-gooders—Roger Ashley in *The Eighth Day* comes to mind as a somewhat less officious but similar type—he tends to be pretentious, pedantic, even patronizing in his efforts to help others. He often adopts the role of schoolmaster in its less flattering aspects, lecturing or directing others with annoying self-assurance and complacency. We are never quite certain that North and the author aren't the same person, so we can't be sure that North is drawn with ironic detachment, as Brush is, and permitted to display his own weaknesses. The narrator conveys the feeling that we are to take him, his good-boy notions, and his actions without irony, that he is really Wilder's alter ego whom we should identify with in his superior wisdom about life and how it should be lived. With that feeling, one inevitably loses sympathy with him and resents his idea of fun, which too often resembles meddling. Sometimes, indeed, North's cleverness in mending character flaws is as objectionable as the flaw itself. When he "cures" young Charles Fenwick of his snobbishness, for instance, North's genteel smugness is almost too much to tolerate, his superior wisdom sounds sententious, and his psychological manipulations are tinged with superciliousness. We expect a man of such sophisticated insights and sensitivity to irony (as he demonstrates in telling us of his "Nine Ambitions") to exhibit a good deal less priggishness about his achievements.

Wilder's failure to handle the narrative point of view with sufficient detachment and irony distorts his purposes by undercutting the value of North's good deeds, but the parts of the book are better than the whole, and if North himself sometimes comes off—unintentionally, we have to think—as a grown-up boy scout, the characters in the episodes are more often than not very engaging. From the brilliant young Eloise Fenwick, sister of Charles, who wants to become a nun, to the selfless, simple Alice, whose only wish is to have North's baby for the sake of her infertile sailor husband—but worries about the immorality of it—all the characters display depths of humanity that raise them above the conventionalism and orthodoxy that stifle freedom and the full enjoyment of life in Newport. North, despite his flaws as a character, serves Wilder well as a kind of lighthearted, sensitive humanist-in-action, a participant in life whose *joie de vivre* is charged by his education in the Classics, his fluency in several languages, his background in archaeology and history. He brings to Newport an awareness of its past (he parallels its "nine cities" with Schliemann's Troy) and a sense of freedom from the restraints of moral and social conformity. His sympathetic involvements often help young persons avoid mistakes, and older people to throw off inhibitions or obstacles to freedom. He succeeds in his desire to restore his own emotional well-being by becoming a helpful friend to others.

His last two novels fairly represent, respectively, the serious and the light sides of Wilder, but his final one is calculated to be a kind of literary festival, a happy affirmation of life. Like his other works, it is indubitably his, and if, as Wilder wished, the reader can join in North's fun—and in his desire to be "obliging"—he or she can enjoy this series of episodes by an author who enjoyed life himself and wanted most touchingly to help his fellow human beings enjoy it, too. Judged against the most demanding standards, the book has some serious narrative problems; but read for amusement and with a slight suspension of critical consciousness, it can provide some amusement, some suspense, some concern for its characters, and some appreciation of its narrator's efforts to show how he had some fun one summer when he was young.

CHAPTER 7

Limitations and Achievement

I N his admirable "reappraisal" of Wilder in *The American Scholar* (spring 1959), Edmund Fuller wrote "in [Wilder's] shrewd, sometimes caustic observation of *genus homo* and his history, we find one of the most searching, balanced and mature visions of ourselves as Man that any American writer offers us." In an article in the *Atlantic Monthly*, Archibald MacLeish declared: "There is no man in America . . . whose words will carry farther around the earth" than Wilder's.[1] These judgments represent, generally, the position still taken by most of Wilder's admirers. They emphasize the quality of his total view of mankind and what it offers to the contemplation of the human condition and not the aesthetic qualities of his works. Critics unfavorably impressed by his efforts have found them sentimental and middle-brow. Viewed from outside Wilder's aesthetic and philosophical assumptions and atmosphere, the weaknesses of his art are obvious enough; and, because they are so apparent, it is perhaps well to begin a summation of his achievement by indicating what they are.

Built upon moral, religious and metaphysical ideas, Wilder's works often lack the narrative and dramatic richness that results when characters respond to complex social, economic, political, or psychological conditions. This problem is more apparent in his plays, which are for the most part allegorical, than in his novels; and it is more obvious in *The Woman of Andros* than in any of the other novels. Because of his effort to give the single instance universal significance, Wilder frequently neglects to make his relation of the single instance sufficiently inclusive. Thus the melancholy of Chrysis in *The Woman* seems maudlin because the soul-deadening conventionalism which is one of her principal antagonists is not fully developed in concrete action.

Wilder's vision is most satisfyingly inclusive as a rule where his characters define themselves through objectively, or "scenically," presented conflict. The fact that *Heaven's My Destination* is a more successful novel than *The Woman of Andros* is explained by the dynamic plot of *Heaven's My Destination* in which George Brush's principles are put into action and tested by specific social obstacles that present the most formidable challenge to the traditional moral and religious values the book affirms. In this novel, moral affirmations arise by implication from the action—and not through the direct statements that characterize *The Woman*. The superiority of *The Ides of March* over *The Woman* can be explained in the same terms. In both books the conflicts are largely inner; but while the interior monologues of Caesar either arise out of action—life as he observes it—or result in action, the inner lives of Chrysis and Pamphilus of *The Woman* consist mainly of melancholy reflections about what life means—with little in the way of dramatic incident as a basis of the reflections.

As we might expect, where the inclusiveness of a fully developed conflict is absent, Wilder achieves his moral and religious affirmations too easily. Antrobus in *The Skin of Our Teeth* survives the disasters that beset mankind, but most of mankind is destroyed by them; and we see no real suffering during his times of crisis. Granting that moral courage and a sense of humor can help minimize the tyranny of circumstance, we do not see Antrobus' courage tested in serious conflict on the stage, and the comedy—sometimes slapstick—largely negates the serious themes. Again, in *The Alcestiad* it is no real struggle for Alcestis to conquer the plague. Acting as if by impulse, she sends her son and his companion for some sulphur with which to purify the drinking water and thereby saves her people from disease. The serious problems of life, we feel while observing Alcestis solve this one, are likely to be more formidable. This is not to say that the problems of modern man cannot be dealt with in an ancient setting. Sartre's *The Flies*, for example, pictures man at odds with powerful social forces that deny his freedom. But whereas Sartre draws clearly and powerfully the antagonists to Orestes—Zeus, Aegistheus, and finally Electra—Wilder fails to provide a well-defined human antagonist to Alcestis; and, with the absence of a visible struggle such as Orestes undergoes, her victory seems too easy. These are Wilder's greatest weaknesses.

The best qualities of his art appear where he wrests his affirmations from a fully developed moral conflict and when they are gained through irony—through a conflict in which moral or religious skepticism appears to gain justification but is undermined by a portrayal of great human spiritual depth and nobility. His best works from this standpoint of conflict are *The Bridge, Heaven's My Destination, The Ides of March, Our Town,* and *The Eighth Day,* where death or apparent defeat place the moral affirmation in bold relief. Less satisfactory are *The Woman, The Skin of Our Teeth,* and *The Alcestiad,* in which themes are stated directly and arbitrarily either by dialogue or, particularly in *The Alcestiad,* through non-realistic action that leaves no moral option for those who cannot accept the mystical nature of the affirmation.

When irony enriches the affirmations through qualification and understatement, Wilder's vision is most compelling. Much of the dramatic impact of *Our Town,* for example, consists in the fact that life in Grover's Corners is at once beautiful and banal. The simple life as lived by the archetypal George and Emily is priceless, but Wilder offers the village drunk—a frustrated musician—as evidence that it can be deadly to talented and sensitive people. In *The Bridge,* the ironic transformation of a religious question into a moral one provides an optional interpretation for both believers and non-believers; in *Heaven's My Destination,* the humanistic position arises by ironic implication from the dialectical conflict between the humanitarian Brush and the materialistic society he encounters; and in *The Ides of March,* the "possibility of mystery" in life subverts Ceasar's skepticism.

Wilder's view of life is less optimistic than it seems, but he has incurred the charge of unwarranted optimism mainly because of those works—most notably *The Skin of Our Teeth*—in which the full force of the dark side of his vision fails to show itself. Except for *Theophilus North* and *The Matchmaker,* none of his novels or full-length plays ends "happily." From *The Cabala* to *The Eighth Day,* and from *Our Town* to *The Alcestiad,* his works end in death for one or another of the major characters, or in grief, or in an unsuccessful attempt to make the world better. His characters typically feel the sting of defeat; and, if they do not always show their suffering as movingly as they might (as movingly, say, as Emily does in Act III of *Our Town*), it is usually because they have come, like Chrysis in *The Woman,* to "accept from the gods all things, the bright and the dark." There is, therefore, a good deal of resignation in Wilder's characters.

The saints are those who, like Madre Maria in *The Bridge* and Alcestis, affirm that life has meaning and do what they can to give it significance, accept the essentially tragic nature of life, and bring

hope to a suffering humanity. Committed to responsibility for eas-
ing the suffering of their fellowmen, they point the way with love,
mercy, tolerance, and understanding for those who cannot help
themselves or are in despair.

But while the courageous ones are Job-like in their praise of life,
despite its apparent meaninglessness, others suffer and cause suffering through insensibility. Lack of sensitivity to other human
beings—particularly the failure to respond to love with love—is the
greatest cause of suffering and, therefore, the greatest source of
tragedy in Wilder's world. Her mother's failure to "realize life"
through consciousness of those closest to her is the cause of Emily's
heartbroken imprecations in Act III of *Our Town*. Cardinal Vaini
and Blair in *The Cabala*, Dona Clara and Camila Perichole in *The
Bridge*, Clodia Pulcher in *The Ides of March*, and *Breckenridge
Lansing in The Eighth Day* all bring spiritual devastation because
of coldness or indifference to those who love them. With the exception of Blair and Dona Clara, these characters are fully and convincingly developed and the full impact of their insensibility is felt in
the profound grief of those who love them. Less effective are such
antagonists as Sostrata and Chremes of *The Woman*, whose preoc-
cupation with social convention is inadequately expressed in action,
and Cain in *The Skin of Our Teeth*, whose evil is caused after all by
misunderstanding.

But while Wilder is less optimistic than he is usually considered
to be and his best works include a full measure of human suffering,
his view is an affirmative one that does not look with despair at the
human condition in the twentieth century. On the contrary, his
message is always that life is a miraculous gift to be cherished and
enjoyed. While he has no sentimental illusions about the innate
goodness of human beings, he is a yea-sayer, like Emerson and
Whitman, who looks kindly upon the foibles of his fellow mortals
and reprehends their bad conduct but believes that their lives on
earth have meaning His *raison d'être* as a writer was always to
point the way, to convey to his audiences and readers his own faith
in the value and meaning of life. Except metaphorically, as in *The
Alcestiad*, supernaturalism does not appear in his work; churches
do, but only as institutions with no particular claims to right or virtue. For Wilder, God's presence is seen in the life-rituals, the
customs, traditions, and values that tie human beings ("Blessed Be
the Tie That Binds") to each other and to their racial past. Those
ties are the basis for faith that somehow humanity, led by its secular
saints, will muddle through and survive.

When Wilder satirizes, he does it gently in the Horatian rather than the Juvenalian, Swiftian manner. Satire is the tool of the skeptic which, used rightly, serves to correct the excesses of faith and sentiment as well as the vices of society. Unchecked skepticism easily deteriorates into cynicism, the denial of faith, and while cynics such as the intellectual Burkin in *Heaven's My Destination* appear as characters on occasion, they are presented without irony. Those like Breckenridge Lansing who use others or are cold before the promptings of the human heart are also cynics. Wilder lets their actions speak for themselves and wastes little sympathy or humor on them. His satire is directed instead toward the naive or gullible, like George Brush; the misguided, like Lily Sabina; the prudish and respectable, like Mrs. Antrobus; and the pompous, like Vandergelder; all of whom are subjected to a laughing satire not unmixed with compassion, tolerance, and promise for reform. The Stage Manager in *Our Town* observes that, "Wherever you come near the human race, there's layers and layers of nonsense," and it is nonsense, absurdity, that Wilder has the most fun with.

Sex plays a relatively unimportant role in either the novels or the plays chiefly because of Wilder's sophisticated acceptance of what his Caesar calls "the fires that populate the earth" and not because of any prudish aversion or denial of its powers in human lives. The Freudian revolution did not bypass Wilder, and he did not reject it or Freud; indeed, he was a personal friend of Freud, who read his works with approval, and there is plenty of evidence, especially in his novels, that he dismissed Victorian sexual moralism as another type of denial of life. Rather, his interests lay elsewhere, in the myriad "forces"—not excluding sex—that create civilizations and civilized individuals. Fuller's statement that Wilder's vision is one of the "most searching, balanced and mature" offered by any American writer is most certainly true in the sense that Wilder avoided the reductive social and psychological-biological determinism found in so much twentieth-century fiction and drama and never subscribed to the "life is hell" school of writing that still dominates American literature. His Caesar asks the questions that concerned Wilder as a novelist and dramatist: "Man—what is that? What do we know of him? His Gods, liberty, mind, love, destiny, death—what do these mean?" Courage before the unalterable circumstances of life and responsibility for alleviating the suffering of one's fellowmen—these are the moral imperatives repeated in his works. They are the indispensable elements in a meaningful, fruitful, and happy life; and it is for a full, free participation in and realization of life that Wilder appeals above all else.

But what, it is pertinent to ask, is the philosophical tradition from which his view of life and the world draws intellectual authority? As Henry James said, "The great question as to a poet or a novelist is, How does he feel about life? What, in the last analysis, is his philosophy? When vigorous writers have reached maturity, we are at liberty to gather from their works some expression of a total view of the world they have been so actively observing. This is the most interesting thing their works offer us." Wilder's "total view" is that of a humanist, but, although he shared the humanistic temperament with Irving Babbitt and Paul Elmer More, he avoided their tendencies to make humanism a dogmatic, systematic philosophy. Moreover, because he appeals for a full, free participation in life, he confronts the logical implications of humanism more satisfactorily than Babbitt and More did. Edmund Wilson justly criticized Babbitt and More because they assumed "that virtue is identical with the will to refrain." To Wilder, such moral and ethical virtues as love, duty, responsibility, justice, and mercy represent positive commitments to life in action and presuppose the full response to, and development of, the passions as well as the ethical conscience. There is less of the spirit of Calvinism in Wilder than in Babbitt and More—particularly in respect to the "lower nature," which he does not despise as they did. He agrees substantially with his Caesar that "to deny that one is an animal is to reduce oneself to half a man," and he avoids what Joseph Wood Krutch in *The Modern Temper* called the "paradox of humanism": its tendency to deplore the very life from which the art it values so highly draws its materials.

But while Wilder does not go so far in approving response to the appetites as, for instance, Hemingway, who declares in effect that whatever pleases or satisfies the senses is good, he does advocate freedom from physical restraints that impoverish or bind the spirit. In this he is more in accord with the Greek doctrine of moderation than the leaders of the Humanist movement were. Furthermore, he holds that what he calls the "wandering desires" and "blind impulses" (the "flux" was More's inclusive term for them) may have a higher meaning than they appear to have and that even the trivial events of everyday life are important. As his Caesar observes, "our lives are immersed in the trivial; the significant comes to us enwrapped in multitudinous details of the trivial; the trivial has this dignity that it exists and is omnipresent." Such a view permits him to affirm that—although its dark counterpart is admitted—"there is no part of the universe that is untouched by bliss."

Unlike such humanists as More and T. S. Eliot, Wilder never identified himself openly with organized religion. But Protestantism, stripped of its sectarian colorations, lies at the heart of his mysticism. His theologian brother, Amos N. Wilder, wrote extensively about the "Reformation Principle" of freedom and responsibility,[2] a principle that is stated or implied in all of Wilder's novels and plays and holds the individual to be free to make his own moral choices without reference to church or state authority but with full responsibility for them in accordance with such Christian moral precepts as love, humility, mercy, and charity. The chief consequence of the principle is that each person is responsible for finding and developing those moral qualities within himself or herself. Examples of this traditional Protestant reliance upon the judgment and reason of the individual are almost too numerous to mention, but one notably direct statement of it appears in *The Ides of March* when Caesar says concerning the rites of the Good Goddess, "Let each woman find out in herself her own goddess—that should be the meaning of these rites." And it is implicit in Wilder's comment in his foreword to *Three Plays:* "Each individual's assertion to an absolute reality can only be inner, very inner."

But in addition to being anchored in the Protestant-humanistic belief in individual responsibility, Wilder's unflagging faith in the value and purpose of life is grounded in his conviction that the family encompasses the traditional values of love, sacrifice, and concern for others; and the rituals and rites of courtship, marriage, and death tie past, present, and future together, and individuals to each other. His affirmative portrayals of males and females in the "roles" that customs and traditions have placed them in admittedly contain stereotyping that seems, in this age when roles and stereotyping are vigorously rejected, somewhat dated and vaguely patronizing; yet they are no less accurate despite the changes in attitudes toward the family and the roles assigned to men and women. But while the family remains for Wilder the basic unit by which civilized societies preserve and pass along their oldest and best values, it is nevertheless the remarkable individuals both within and outside families who articulate and practice the highest moral values and lead the way in every generation; a substantial number of those remarkable persons are women.

In his eclecticism, his view of life that is grounded in New England Protestantism but encompasses "the best that has been thought and said" in the literary past—and has room for thought as diverse as the ethical humanism of Jean-Paul Sartre and the

religious existentialism of Sören Kierkegaard and Nicholas Berdyaev—Wilder belongs in the tradition of moralists and teachers
that includes Emerson, Theodore Parker, and Amos Bronson Alcott,
who also drew upon European and Oriental as well as native
American intellectual currents during the nineteenth century. At his
comic best, he is descended from Voltaire, Sheridan, and
Goldsmith—eighteenth-century European and English humor—more than from any American writers. But, different as Walt
Whitman's stylistic superabundance is from Wilder's almost
Classical economy, Whitman, with his exuberant but not unmixed
optimism about the possibilities of the common man and culture in
a democratic society, is Wilder's true American literary ancestor.
Self-reliance; the infinite worth of individuals; the nursing of
idiosyncracies which save them from conformity and enable them to
define and realize their purpose according to their nature; full
development of the mental and physical powers, of conscience and
the religious sense (without churches); full political participation
without commitment to party; and the highest realization of the intrinsic qualities and dignity of womanhood—these were some of
Whitman's proposals for the perfection of individual persons and of
American democracy. Like Wilder, Whitman maintained that the
ideas literature conveys provide its primary justification and purpose. "The culmination and fruit of literary artistic expression,"
Whitman wrote in a footnote to "Democratic Vistas," "and its final
fields of pleasure for the human soul, are in metaphysics, including
the mysteries of the spiritual world, the soul itself, and the question
of the immortal continuation of our identity."

From the bedside of the dying Catullus, Caesar, in *The Ides of
March*, writes: "I am no stranger to deathbeds. To those in pain one
talks about themselves; to those of clear mind one praises the world
that they are quitting. There is no dignity in leaving a despicable
world and the dying are often fearful lest life was not worth the efforts it had cost them. I am never short of subjects to praise." Like
Whitman, Wilder above all else affirmed the dignity of man and the
priceless value of life. Unlike most major writers of his time he did
not point to the meanness, pettiness, and animalism of man. No
Apeneck Sweeneys, Popeyes, or Congo Jakes, inhabit his world. He
always maintained that no attitude or doctrine which debases the
human individual by pointing to his depravity or to his helplessness
can lead men to salvation. If men are insensitive, cruel, and
animalistic and if they are brutalized or driven to despair by

necessity or circumstance, it is the responsibility of those of cultivated sensibility and intelligence to bring the force of wisdom and courage to bear upon the suffering that results—to show the way in understanding and sympathy, as do Madre Maria, Chrysis, Caesar, Alcestis, and even George Brush, who is working his way toward that wisdom. There is little men can do to eliminate evil and circumstance, but they can reduce with moral courage and faith the power of those forces, keep the spark of humanity alive in the world, and carve out for themselves a meaningful and happy existence.

In an article on James Joyce (*Poetry*, March 1941), Wilder wrote: "The price that must be paid for a love that cannot integrate its hate is sentimentality; the price that must be paid for a hate that cannot integrate its love is, variously, empty rhetoric, insecurity of taste, and the sterile refinements of an intellect bent on destruction." Wilder occasionally paid the price of sentimentality. But he was never guilty of empty rhetoric, insecurity of taste or intellectual destructiveness; and this accomplishment was unusual in a literary era when it was fashionable to be esoteric or iconoclastic, when a dim view of humanity was virtually a dogma and when a writer supposedly lacked depth unless he was in despair.

Wilder's view is a mature one, as Fuller said, because it is the product of a balanced personality whose love and hate were successfully integrated. He accepted the moral responsibilities of the humanist; and, because he consistently affirmed the dignity and worth not only of the individual person but also of American democracy, he became as MacLeish pointed out, one of the most powerful living American spokesmen for the humanistic values his country was founded upon. To admit that the nation has largely forgotten those values does not deny their validity or the merit of trying to restore them in the nation's conscience and, by implication, to the hearts and minds of human beings everywhere. Wilder, unlike such of his contemporaries as T. S. Eliot, wrote of and for the millions; and while at times—as in *The Skin of Our Teeth*—he admittedly descended into bathos and didacticism, he also gave fresh expression to the best and most enduring values of humanity. Though his works are less esoteric than some critics would have liked them to be, they seem likely to continue bringing enjoyment and intellectual stimulation to large audiences of readers and viewers long after many of our more esoteric and topical contemporary novels and plays have died quietly on library shelves.

Notes and References

Preface

1. "Why Is a Best-Seller?" *Outlook*, CXLVIII (April 18, 1928) 643.
2. Adcock, "Thornton Wilder," *The Bookman*, LXXV (March 1929), 316 - 19.
3. "Thornton Wilder to the Front," *Literary Digest* (April 21, 1928), 25 - 26.
4. Quoted by Salpeter, *Outlook*, 634.
5. Hazlitt, "Communist Criticism," CXXXI (November 26, 1930), 583 - 84.
6. Wilson, "The Economic Interpretation of Wilder," LXV (November 26, 1930), 31 - 32. (Unsigned article later published in *The Shores of Light.*)
7. Cowley, *Exile's Return* (New York: The Viking Press, 1951),
8. Cf. Richard Goldstone's *Thornton Wilder: An Intimate Portrait* (New York: Saturday Review Press / E. P. Dutton & Co., Inc., 1975), and Cowley's review of Goldstone's volume in the *New York Times Book Review*, November 9, 1975, 6 - 7. Goldstone's response to the Cowley review and Cowley's rejoinder are in the December 21, 1975, issue of the *Times Book Review*, p. 20.

Chapter One

1. "An Obliging Man," *Time*, LXI (January 12, 1953), 45.
2. See Malcolm Cowley's *Exile's Return* for a full treatment of the "Lost Generation" and the reasons for their self-imposed isolation.
3. Cf. Richard Goldstone, *Thornton Wilder: An Intimate Portrait* (New York: Saturday Review Press / E. P. Dutton & Co., Inc., 1975), p. 52. Goldstone's analysis of Hemingway and Wilder in Chapter 5 is fascinating, if at times conjectural.
4. More, *On Being Human* (Princeton: Princeton University Press, 1928) III, New Shelburne Essays.
5. From *Selected Essays: 1917 - 1932* by T. S. Eliot, copyright, 1932, by Harcourt, Brace and Company, Inc., 1932; renewed, 1960, by T. S. Eliot. Reprinted by permission of the publishers.
6. More, *On Being Human*, pp. 19 - 20.

Chapter Two

1. "Thornton Wilder," *Literary Chronicle: 1920 - 1950*, 103.

2. *Ibid.*

3. Quoted by Parmenter, "Novelist into Playwright," *Saturday Review of Literature* (June 11, 1938), 10 - 11.

4. Quoted by Walther Tritsch, "Thornton Wilder in Berlin," *The Living Age*, CCXLIX (September 1931), 46.

5. See *A Grammar of Motives*, (New York: Prentice-Hall, Inc., 1952). The terms "extrinsic motivations" and "intrinsic motivations" are borrowed from Burke and are used as nearly as possible in the same sense he uses them.

6. See Walther Fischer, "*The Bridge of San Luis Rey* und Prosper Merimee's *La Carosse Du Saint-Sacrement*," *Anglia-Zeitschrift für Englische Philologie*, Band LX, Heft 11/2 (January 1936).

7. See Bruce Harkness, "The Epigraph in Conrad's Chance," *Nineteenth Century Fiction*, IX (December 1954), 209 - 22.

8. Kenneth Burke and Stanley Romaine Hopper, "Mysticism as a Solution to the Poet's Dilemma," *Spiritual Problems in Contemporary Literature* (New York: Harper and Brothers, 1952), 105.

9. Parmenter, "Novelist into Playwright," 11.

Chapter Three

1. Tritsch, "Thornton Wilder in Berlin," *The Living Age*, CCCXLIX (September 1931), 47.

2. Introduction to *Three Plays* (New York: Harper and Brothers, 1957), xii.

3. Gassner, *Form and Idea in Modern Theatre*, (New York: Holt, Rinehart and Winston, 1956), pp. 141 - 42. Gassner says: "The fundamental premise of realism is the Aristotelian one that drama is an imitation of an action; realists held, therefore, that the most desirable theatre is that in which imitation is closest. The fundamental premise of theatricalism is that theatre is not imitation in the narrow sense, which Aristotle never could have held, since the Greek drama upon which he based conclusions in his *Poetics* was not realistically imitative. For the theatricalist, the object of action and of all other 'imitative' elements is not imitation but *creativeness*, and a special kind of creativeness at that. The realists would agree, of course, as to the value of creativeness. But the theatricalist goes one step further, and that step is the truly decisive one for the theory and practice of pure theatricalism. He maintains that there is never any sense in pretending that one is not in the theatre; that no amount of make-believe is reality itself; that in short, theatre is the medium of dramatic art, and the effectiveness in art consists in *using* the medium rather than concealing it."

4. Introduction to *Three Plays*, xi.

5. Tritsch, 47.

6. Parmenter, "Novelist into Playwright," 10 - 11.

7. See Dayton Kohler, "Thornton Wilder," *English Journal*, XXVII (January 1939), 6.

Chapter Four

1. See esp. Wilder's introduction to *Geographical History of America* by Gertrude Stein (New York: Random House, 1936).
2. See "An Obliging Man," *Time* (January 12, 1953), 46.
3. Introduction to *Geographical History of America*, 13.
4. (Princeton: Princeton University Press, 1941.)
5. Introduction to *Geographical History of America*, 21.
6. See "Three Allegorists: Brecht, Wilder and Eliot," in Fergusson's *The Human Image in Dramatic Literature* (New York: Doubleday Anchor Books, 1957), 41 - 71.
7. Brown, "Wilder: *Our Town*," *Saturday Review of Literature* (August 6, 1949), 34.
8. T. S. Eliot: *The Design of His Poetry* (New York: Charles Scribner's Sons, 1949), 101.
9. *The Nation*, CLXXVI (December 4, 1955), 562.
10. See esp. "James Joyce (1888 - 1941)," *Poetry: A Magazine of Verse*, LVII (March 1941), 370 - 74.
11. Part I, XXV (December 19, 1942), 3.
12. See Robinson's "The Strange Case of Thornton Wilder," *Esquire*, XLVII (March 1957), 71, 124 - 26.
13. See Wilson's "The Antrobuses and the Earwickers," *The Nation*, CLVI (January 30, 1943), 167 - 68.
14. "The Skin of Whose Teeth?" Part II, *Saturday Review of Literature* (December 26, 1942), 11.
15. *Time*, XL (December 28, 1942), 62.
16. Cf. Wilson's "The Antrobuses and the Earwickers" (note 13 above) for the most convincing expression of this view.
17. See Gassner's *Form and Idea in Modern Theatre*, p. 143. Gassner maintains that *Skin* is the best theatricalist play in American theatre, except for Cummings' dadaist-surrealist play *him*.

Chapter Five

1. "Existentialism and Humanism," translated with an Introduction by Philip Mairet (London: Mathuen and Company, Ltd., 1949). (French ed. first published in 1946).
2. Quoted by Paul M. Cubeta, *Modern Drama for Analysis* (New York: Holt, Rinehart and Winston, Inc., 1955), 595 - 96.
3. Quoted from Berdyaev's *Dream and Reality* by F. H. Heineman in *Existentialism and the Modern Temper* (New York: Harper and Brothers, 1958), 161.

Chapter Six

1. Seven one-act plays were projected for each of the two cycles.

"Childhood" (*Atlantic Monthly* November 1960, 78 - 84) is the only one published thus far.

Chapter Seven

1. MacLeish, "The Isolation of the American Artist," *The Atlantic Monthly*, CCI (January 1958), 59.

2. See esp. *Spiritual Aspects of the New Poetry* (New York: Harper and Brothers, 1940).

Selected Bibliography

PRIMARY SOURCES

The Trumpet Shall Sound. In *Yale Literary Magazine* (October 1919 to January 1920 inclusive).

"A Diary: First and Last Entry," *S4N* (February 1924).

"Three Sentences." *Double Dealer* (September 1924).

The Cabala. New York: Albert and Charles Boni, Inc., 1926.

The Bridge of San Luis Rey. New York: Albert and Charles Boni,, Inc., 1927.

The Angel That Troubled the Waters. New York: Coward-McCann, Inc., 1928.

"Playgoing Nights: From a Travel Diary," *Theatre Arts Monthly,* XIII (June 1929), 411 - 19. (Written in collaboration with Isabel Wilder.)

The Woman of Andros. New York: Albert and Charles Boni, Inc., 1930.

The Long Christmas Dinner and Other Plays in One Act. New York: Coward-McCann, Inc., 1931.

Lucrèce (adapted from the French original of André Obey). Boston: Houghton Mifflin, 1933.

Heaven's My Destination: New York: Harper and Brothers, 1935.

Introduction to *Narration: Four Lectures* by Gertrude Stein. Chicago: University of Chicago Press, 1935, v - viii.

Our Town. New York: Harper and Brothers, 1935.

Introduction to *The Geographical History of America* by Gertrude Stein. New York: Random House, 1936.

"The Warship." *Yale Literary Magazine* (February 1936), 64 - 67.

The Merchant of Yonkers. New York: Harper and Brothers, 1939.

"James Joyce (1882 - 1941)," *Poetry: A Magazine of Verse,* LVII (March 1941), 370 - 74.

"Some Thoughts on Playwrighting," in *The Intent of the Artist,* ed. Augusto Centeno (Princeton: Princeton University Press, 1941), 83 - 98.

The Skin of Our Teeth. New York: Harper and Brothers, 1942.

Our Century. New York: Century Association, 1947.

The Ides of March. New York: Harper and Brothers, 1948.

"World Literature and the Modern Mind," in *Goethe and the Modern Age,* ed. Arnold Bergstrasser (Chicago: Henry Regnery Company, 1949), 213 - 24.

"Fraternity of Man." *Time* LVIII (July 2, 1951), 61. (Report of Wilder's Commencement Address at Harvard, June 1951.)

"Toward an American Language." *The Atlantic Monthly*, CLXXXX (July 1952), 29 - 37.

"The American Loneliness," *The Atlantic Monthly*, CLXXXX (August 1952), 65 - 69.

"Emily Dickinson." *The Atlantic Monthly*, CLXXXX (November 1952), 43 - 48.

"Silent Generation." *Harpers*, CCVI (April 1953), 34 - 36.

The Matchmaker. New York: Harper and Brothers, 1955. (Revision of *The Merchant of Yonkers*.)

Introduction to *Oedipus the King* by Sophocles. New York: Heritage, 1955.

Three Plays: Our Town, The Skin of Our Teeth, The Matchmaker, with a preface by Wilder. New York: Harper, 1957.

"The Drunken Sisters." *Atlantic Monthly* (November 1957), 92 - 95. (The satyr play for *The Alcestiad*.)

"Kultur in Einer Demokratie." In *Thornton Wilder*. Frankfort Am Main: Börsenverein des Deutschen Buchshandels E. V., 1957.

"Childhood." *Atlantic Monthly* (November 1960) 78 - 84.

The Alcestiad. Translated from English into German by H. E. Herlitschka. Frankfurt: Fischer Bucherei, 1960.

The Eighth Day. New York: Harper and Row, 1967.

Theophilus North. New York: Harper and Row, 1973.

The Alcestiad. New York: Harper and Row, 1977.

SECONDARY SOURCES

1. Criticism of Wilder's Work

BROWN, E. K. "A Christian Humanist." *University of Toronto Quarterly*, IV (April 1935), 356 - 70.

BROWN, JOHN MASON. "Wilder: *Our Town*." *Saturday Review of Literature* (August 6, 1949), 32 - 34.

CAMPBELL, JOSEPH and HENRY M. ROBINSON. "The Skin of Whose Teeth?" *Saturday Review of Literature*, XXV (February 13, 1943), 16 - 18. The attack on Wilder for unacknowledged use of materials from Jorce's *Finnegans Wake*.

CORRIGAN, ROBERT W. "Thornton Wilder and the Tragic Sense of Life." Educational Theater, XIII (October 1961), 167 - 73.

COWLEY, MALCOLM. Introduction to *A Thornton Wilder Trio*. New York: Criterion Books, Inc., 1956. This excellent article is a must for all readers of Wilder, for it relates how he differs from his contemporaries in his use of moral themes and in his historical perspective; it was also published earlier in a slightly longer form as "The Man Who Abolished Time" in *SRL* (October 6, 1956), 13 - 14, 50 - 52.

DAVIS, ELMER, "Caesar's Last Months." *Saturday Review of Literature*, XXXI (February 21, 1948), 11 - 12.

EDGELL, DAVID P. "Thornton Wilder Revisited." *Cairo Studies in English*, II (1960), 47 - 59.

FERGUSSON, FRANCIS. "Three Allegorists: Brecht, Wilder and Eliot," *The Sewanee Review*, LXIV (Autumn 1956), 544 - 73. Reprinted in Fergusson's *The Human Image in Dramatic Literature* (New York: Doubleday Anchor Books, 1957), 41 - 71. Points to lack of historical dimension as major weakness of Wilder's dramatic work.

FIREBAUGH, JOSEPH. "The Humanism of Thornton Wilder," *The Pacific Spectator*, IV (Autumn 1950), 426 - 28. One of the best works on Wilder to date, this article defines Wilder's humanism broadly in terms of recurrent themes.

Four Quarters. Special Wilder Issue, XVI (May 1967). Articles by Hans Sahl, Joseph Firebaugh, Isabel Wilder, Richard Goldstone, Donald Haberman, R. W. Stallman.

FULLER, EDMUND. "Reappraisals: Thornton Wilder: 'The Notation of the Heart,'" *The American Scholar*, XXVIII (Spring 1959), 210 - 17. Evaluates Wilder's achievement and places him among the great writers of our time on the basis of his complex and mature vision.

GOLD, MICHAEL. "Wilder: Prophet of the Genteel Christ." *New Republic*, LXIV (October 22, 1930), 266 - 67.

GOLDSTEIN, MALCOLM. *The Art of Thornton Wilder*. Omaha, Nebraska: The University of Nebraska Press, 1965.

GOLDSTONE, RICHARD. "An Interview with Thornton Wilder." *Paris Review*, XV (Winter, 1957), 36 - 57.

_____. "Of a Quality That Lasts." *New York Times Book Review* (June 20, 1965), 1.

_____. *Thornton Wilder: An Intimate Portrait*. New York: Saturday Review Press / E. P. Dutton & Co. Inc., 1975.

GREBANIER, BERNARD. *Thornton Wilder*. Minneapolis: University of Minnesota Press, 1964.

GUTHRIE, TYRONE. "The World of Thornton Wilder," *New York Times Magazine* (November 27, 1955), 26 - 27, 64, 66 - 68. A perceptive survey of Wilder's vision by a man who has directed some of Wilder's plays.

HABERMAN, DONALD. *The Plays of Thornton Wilder*. Middletown, Connecticut: Wesleyan University Press, 1967.

HEWITT, BARNARD. "Thornton Wilder Says 'Yes.'" *Tulane Drama Review*, IV (December 1959), 110 - 20.

KOHLER, DAYTON, "Thornton Wilder," *English Journal*, XXVIII (January 1939), 1 - 11. Particularly good appraisal of Wilder's style.

MACLEISH, ARCHIBALD. "The Isolation of the American Artist." *Atlantic Monthly*, CCI (January 1958), 55 - 59.

MCNAMARA, ROBERT. "Phases of American Religion in Thornton Wilder and Willa Cather," *The Catholic World*, CXXXV (September 1932), 641 - 49. Traces Wilder's early attempts to remind Americans of their religious heritage.

NELSON, ROBERT. "An Obliging Man." *Time*, LXI (January 12, 1953), 44 - 49.

PAPAJEWSKI, HELMUT. *Thornton Wilder*. New York: Frederick Ungar, 1968.

PARMENTER, ROSS. "Novelist into Playwright," *Saturday Review of Literature* (June 11, 1938), 10 - 11. Shows dramatic qualities of early novels as stages in Wilder's development as a dramatist.

POPPER, HERMINE I. "The Universe of Thornton Wilder." *Harper's*, CCXXX (June 1965), 72 - 81.

SALPETER, HARRY. "Why Is a Best-Seller?" *Outlook*, CXLVIII (April 18, 1928), 643.

SCOTT, WINFIELD TOWNLEY. "*Our Town* and the Golden Veil," *Virginia Quarterly Review*, XXIX (January 1953), 103 - 17. Describes the dualistic nature of *Our Town*, the fusion of past and present, natural and supernatural.

SMITH, HARRISON. "The Skin of Whose Teeth?" Part II, *Saturday Review of Literature*, XXV (December 26, 1942), 12.

STÜRZL, ERWIN. "Weltbild und Lebensphilosophie Thornton Wilders," *Die Neueren Sprachen*, Heft 8, 1955, 341 - 51. Shows relationship between Wilder's extensive travel and the universality of his themes.

WESCOTT, GLENWAY. *Images of Truth*. New York: Harper and Row, 1962.

WILSON, EDMUND. "The Antrobuses and the Earwickers," *The Nation*, CXVI (January 30, 1943), 167 - 68. Best appraisal of the *Skin of Our Teeth*-*Finnegans Wake* controversy; justifies Wilder's borrowing from Joyce.

————. "Dahlberg, Dos Passos and Wilder," "Mr. Wilder in the Middle West," "Thornton Wilder," "The Economic Interpretation of Wilder," in *The Shores of Light*. New York: Farrar, Straus and Young, 1952. Perceptive studies of Wilder's first four novels.

————. "Thornton Wilder: The Influence of Proust," *New Republic*, LV (August 8, 1928), 303 - 5.

2. Valuable Background Sources

BENTLEY, ERIC. *The Playwright as Thinker*. New York: Meridian Books, 1957. A thorough treatment of "The two traditions of modern drama": realism and antirealism.

COWLEY, MALCOLM, *Exile's Return*. New York: The Viking Press, 1951. One of the best works on the American literary exiles of the 1920s—the men and women of Wilder's generation.

FULTON, A. R. "Expressionism—Twenty Years After," *Sewanee Review*, LII (Summer 1944), 210 - 17. Notes the expressionistic elements of *Our Town* and *The Skin of Our Teeth*.

GASSNER, JOHN. *Form and Idea in Modern Theatre*. New York: The Dryden Press, 1956. Puts Wilder in the theatricalist tradition of dramaturgy. Indispensable to the understanding of Wilder's place in modern drama.

HOPPER, STANLEY ROMAINE (ed.). *Spiritual Problems in Contemporary Literature*. New York: Harper and Brothers, 1952. See esp. "Mysticism as a Solution to the Poet's Dilemma" by Hopper and Kenneth Burke for insight into Wilder's resolution of the conflict between skepticism and faith.

MORE, PAUL ELMER. *On Being Human* (New Shelburne Essays, III), Princeton: Princeton University Press, 1936. The New Humanism explained by one of its leading figures.

WILDER, AMOS NIVEN. *Spiritual Aspects of the New Poetry*. New York: Harper and Brothers, 1940. The religious point of view in this book is very close to that revealed in Thornton Wilder's work.

Index

(The works of Wilder are listed under his name)

Abbey Theatre, 30
Adding Machine, The (Rice), 31
Aeschylus, 62
Aestheticism, 50, 53, 54
Alcestis (Euripides), 106 - 107
Alcott, A. Bronson, 69, 134
Ambassadors, The (James), 31, 32
American, The (James), 31
American Academy in Rome, 20
American Laboratory Theatre, 20
Andria, The (Terence), 50, 51
Apollinaire, Guillaume, 30
Aristotle, 74, 93, 95
Arnold, Matthew, 27, 67

Babbitt, Irving, 27 - 29, 54, 132
Balzac, Honoré, 28
Bankhead, Tallulah, 87
Becque, Henri, 25, 30
Berdyaev, Nicolas, 111 - 112, 134
Boleslavsky, Richard, 20
Boni, Albert and Charles, 20
Brooks, Cleanth, 63
Brown, John Mason, 80
Browne, Sir Thomas, 41, 42
Bruno, Giordano, neo-Platonism of, 88
Burke, Kenneth, 47

Cabell, James Branch, 31, 32
Caesar, Julius, 97
Campbell, Joseph, controversy over *Skin*, 87 - 88; see also Henry Morton Robinson
Cathleen ni Houlihan (Yeats), 30
Candide (Voltaire), 69
Centeno, Augusto, 71
Central intelligence, 32

Chance (Conrad), 41, 47
Channing, Ellery, 122
Chivalry (Cabell), 31
Claudel, Paul, 30
Clurman, Harold, 83
Cocktail Party, The (Eliot), 107
Cocteau, Jean, 107, 112
Conrad, Joseph, 41, 47
Corneille, Pierre, 74
Cornell, Katharine, 63
Cowley, Malcolm, 52
Crane, Stephen, 39

Dante, 82
Darwinism, 27
Day Well Spent, A (Oxenham), 54
De Bosis, Lauro, 97
"Democratic Vistas" (Whitman), 134
Dos Passos, John, 17, 39, 49
Dream and Reality (Berdyaev), 111 - 112
Dreiser, Theodore, 28, 31, 39
Drew, Elizabeth, 82
Dualism, 46, 70, 79, 88, 91

Einen Jux will er sich Machen (Nestroy), 84
Eliot, T. S., 28, 29, 73, 82, 107, 123, 133, 135
Elmer Gantry (Lewis), 64, 67
Emerson, R. W., 67, 122, 130, 134
Emperor Jones, The (O'Neill), 31
Esquire, 88
Euripides, 106 - 107. See *Alcestis*
"Evening with Thornton Wilder, An," 115
Existentialism, 97, 98; in *The Ides of*

March, 97 - 106; in *The Alcestiad*, 106 - 114
"Existentialism and Humanism" (Sartre), 98
Expressionism, 30, 31, 58

Faulkner, William, 17
Faust (Goethe), epigraph in *The Ides of March*, 100
Fergusson, Francis, 73, 74
Finnegans Wake (Joyce), controversy over *Skin of Our Teeth*, 86 - 89
Fitzgerald, F. Scott, 17, 49
Flies, The (Sartre), 107, 110, 128
Foerster, Norman, 54
Fort Adams, Rhode Island, 20
Frazer, Sir James George, 36, 89. See also, *The Golden Bough*
Freud, Sigmund, 36, 122
Fuller, Edmund, 127, 131

Gassner, John, 58
Gide, Andre, 30
Gold, Michael, 68, 87
Golden Bough, The (Frazer), 89
Golden Bowl, The (James), 30
Goldsmith, Oliver, 134
Goldstone, Richard, 19
Grapes of Wrath, The (Steinbeck), 68
Guthrie, Tyrone, 84

Hebraic-Christian tradition, 25, 28, 122
Hebraism and Hellenism, in *Skin of Our Teeth*, 86 - 96
Hellenic-Christian culture, 32
Hellzapoppin' (Olsen and Johnson), 88, 89
Hemingway, Ernest, 17, 18, 49, 132
Hindemith, Paul, 114, 115
Howells, W. D., 30
Huckleberry Finn (Twain), 69
Humanism, 32, 44, 50, 52, 63, 67, 69, 70, 79, 86; in *Skin of Our Teeth*, 86 - 96; 98, 132. See also New Humanism
Humanitarianism, in *Heaven's My Destination*, 65 - 69

Hutchins, Robert Maynard, 19, 70
Hutchins, William, 19
Huxley, Thomas Henry, 27

Ibsen, Henrik, 25, 30
Infernal Machine, The (Cocteau), 107
Intent of the Artist (Centeno), 71
In Dubious Battle (Steinbeck), 68
Isaacs, Edith, 20

James, Henry, 30, 31, 32, 37, 38, 132
Job theme, 24, 62, 130
Joyce, James, 36, 86 - 89, 123
Jurgen (Cabell), 31, 32

Kennedy, John F., 115
Kierkegaard, Sören, 24, 111, 134
Krutch, Joseph Wood, 132

La Carosse Du Saint Sacrement (Mérimée), 40
Lawrenceville School, 20, 21, 124
Lewis, R. W. B., 122
Lewis, Sinclair, 31, 39, 49, 64, 67
Liberty Theatre, Oakland, Calif., 19
Life Is Real (Rice), 58
Literary schools, 17 - 18
Lost Generation, 17, 32
Lucréce (Obey), 63

MacDowell Colony, 21
MacLeish, Archibald, 127
Maeterlinck, Maurice, 30
Mann, Thomas, 123
Maugham, W. Somerset, 28
Mencken, H. L., 31
Mérimée, Prosper, 40, 50
Modern Temper, The (Krutch), 132
More, Paul Elmer, 27 - 29, 54, 132, 133
Musical structure, 60 - 63
Mysticism, 40, 42, 47, 53, 71, 81; T. S. Eliot on romantic vs. classical, 82; in *The Alcestiad*, 108 - 114
Myth, in *Our Town*, 81 - 83; in *Skin of Our Teeth*, 89

Nathan, George Jean, 87
Naturalism, philosophical, conflict with New Humanism, 27 - 29; 30, 31, 39, 40
Nestroy, Johann, 84
New Humanism, 27 - 29. See also Irving Babbitt and Paul Elmer More
New Orleans *Double Dealer*, 20
Niven, Rev. Thornton M. (grandfather of Thornton Wilder), 18
Non-realism, 30, 31, 55, 56

Oberlin College, 19, 70
Oberlin Literary Magazine, 19
Obey, André, Wilder's translation of *Lucréce*, 63
Oedipus Rex, (Sophocles), 74 - 75
Olsen and Johnson, 88, 89. See also *Hellzapoppin'*
O'Neill, Eugene, 17, 18, 25, 28, 31
Oresteia, The (Aeschylus), 107
"Out of the Cradle Endlessly Rocking" (Whitman) 116
Oxenham, John, 84. See also "A Day Well Spent"

Parker, Theodore, 122, 134
Parmenter, Ross, 53 - 54, 64
Platonism, 21 - 26, 72, 93, 95
Princeton University, 20
Prometheus Myth, 30
Proust, Marcel, 30, 31, 36
Pulitzer Prize, 87
Purgatory (Dante), 75

Quintero, José, 115

Racine, Jean, 174
Rationalism, 32
Realism, 30, 32, 39, 40, 55, 56, 58, 59, 74
Reinhardt, Max, 83
Religious drama, 30
Remembrance of Things Past (Proust), 30
Rice, Elmer, 17, 31, 58

Robinson, Henry Morton, 87 - 88. See also, Joseph Campbell

S4N, 20
Sacred Fount, The (James), 30
Salpeter, Harry, 39
Sartre, Jean-Paul, 98, 107, 110, 112, 128, 133
Satire, 67 - 68, 86, 131
Sessions, Roger, 116
Shakespeare, William, 58
Sheridan, Richard B., 134
Sherwood, Robert, 17
Smith,. Harrison, 87
Spengler, Oswald, 36
Spinoza, Baruch, 93, 95
Stage manager, as dramatic device, 26, 55, 59; in *Our Town*, 76 - 83; in *Skin of Our Teeth*, 88 - 89; in *The Alcestiad*, 107
Stein, Gertrude, 70 - 75, 83
Steinbeck, John, 68. See also *Grapes of Wrath*
Strindberg, August, 25, 30, 58.
Surrealism, 30
Swift, Jonathan, 131
Symbolism, 30, 32

Talma, Louise, 115
Tate, Allen, 63
Terence, 50, 51
Theatre Arts Monthly, 20
Theatricalism, 68, 69, 73, 72 - 75, 76 - 96
Thoreau, Henry D., 68
Time interviews with Wilder, 17, 18, 70, 87 - 88
Tom Jones (Fielding), 69
Tritsch, Walther, 40, 55
"Turn of the Screw, The" (James) 30

University of Chicago, 70
Verisimilitude, 58, 59, 61, 74
Vico, Giambattista, cyclical theory of history, 88
Voltaire, 134

Wager, Charles, 19, 70

"When Lilacs Last in the Dooryard Bloom'd" (Whitman), 116

Whitman, Walt, 28, 83, 116, 122, 130, 134

Wilder, Amos Niven (brother), 18; "Reformàtion Principle," 133

Wilder, Amos P. (father), 18

Wilder, Isabel (sister), 18

Wilder, Isabella (mother), 18

Wilder, Janet (sister), 18

Wilder, Thornton N., as Christian humanist, 18, 21 - 29, 82; early life, 18 - 21; early works, 21 - 26; family in his works, 121, 133; honors and awards, 115 - 116; Masters degree at Princeton, 20; mysticism in his works, 23; religious background, 18; resignation from Lawrenceville School, 21; sentimentalism in his works, 26, 53, 54; Service in World War II, 97; theory of drama, 58, 72 - 75; travels in Europe, 20 - 21

WORKS - DRAMA:

Alcestiad, The, 26, 73, 106 - 114; as opera, 116; 123, 128, 129, 130. See also *Die Alkestiade* and *Life in the Sun*

Alkestiade, Die, 115, 116. See also, *The Alcestiad* and *A Life in the Sun*

Angel That Troubled the Waters, The, 21, 25, 27, 29, 30, 56, 123

"And the Sea Shall Give up Its Dead," 23

"Angel That Troubled the Waters, The," 23

"Centaurs," 22, 89

"Child Roland to the Dark Tower Came," 23

"Fanny Otcott," 24, 29

"Flight into Egypt, The," 23 - 24, 88 - 89

"Hast Thou Considered My Servant Job?" 23, 25

"Leviathan," 23

"Message and Jehanne, The," 26

"Mozart and the Gray Steward," 22, 88

"Nascuntur Poetae," 22

"Now the Servant's Name Was Malchus," 23, 24

"Penny That Beauty Spent, The," 26

"Drunken Sisters, The" (satyr play for *The Alcestiad*), 111

Life in the Sun (The Alcestiad), 111

Long Christmas Dinner and Other Plays in One Act, The, 54, 55 - 63

"Happy Journey to Trenton and Camden, The," 56, 58, 59 - 60, 62, 76

"Long Christmas Dinner, The," 56, 57, 58, 59, 62; as opera, 63; 88, 114, 115

"Love and How to Cure It," 56, 57

"Pullman Car Hiawatha," 26, 56, 58, 60 - 63, 76, 88

"Queens of France," 56

"Such Things Only Happen in Books," 56, 57

Matchmaker, The, 57, 73, 83 - 86, 106, 123, 129. See also *The Merchant of Yonkers*

Merchant of Yonkers, The, 83. See *The Matchmaker*

Our Town, 26, 56, 62, 63, 71, 72, 73, 74, 75 - 83; as religious festival, 82 - 83; 91, 94, 116, 121, 123, 129, 130, 131

Plays for Bleecker Street, 115. See *The Seven Ages of Man* and *The Seven Deadly Sins*

Seven Ages of Man, The, 115, 123

"Childhood," 115

"Infancy," 115

Seven Deadly Sins, The, 115, 123

"Someone from Assisi," 115

Trumpet Shall Sound, The, 20

WORKS - FICTION:

Bridge of San Luis Rey, The, 20, 21, 30, 38, 39 - 49, 50, 51, 57, 88, 98, 102, 106, 113, 117, 123, 129

Cabala, The, 20, 30, 31 - 38, 39, 40, 49, 50, 57, 88, 117, 123, 129, 130

"Diary: First and Last Entry," 20

Eighth Day, The, 106, 115-123, 129, 130

Heaven's My Destination, 63 - 69, 71, 86, 123, 128, 129, 131

Ides of March, The, 97 - 106, 108, 117, 123, 128, 129, 130, 133, 134

Memoirs of a Roman Student (The Cabala), 20

Theophilus North, 123 - 126, 129

"Three Sentences" (from *The Cabala*), 20

Woman of Andros, The, 39, 49 - 54, 63, 68, 106, 123, 127, 128, 129, 130

WORKS - OTHER PROSE:

Introduction to *Four in America* by Gertrude Stein, 70, 71

Introduction to *Geographical History of America* by Gertrude Stein, 70

Introduction to *Narration: Four Lectures* by Gertrude Stein, 70

Introduction to *Oedipus Rex,* 74 - 75

Introduction to *Three Plays,* 58, 75, 84, 87, 133

Wilson, Edmund, 31, 36, 87, 132

Wings of the Dove (James), 30, 31, 37

Wisconsin State Journal, 18

Yale Literary Magazine, 20

Yale University, 18, 19, 20, 70

Yeats, W. B., 30, 123

Zola, Emile, 28, 30